THE PRE-COMPUTER BOOK

ALSO BY THE SAME AUTHOR

No. BP53	Practical Electronics Calculations and Formulae
No. BP62	Elements of Electronics – Book 1 The Simple Electronic Circuit and Components
No. BP63	Elements of Electronics – Book 2 Alternating Current Theory
No. BP64	Elements of Electronics – Book 3 Semiconductor Technology
No. BP77	Elements of Electronics – Book 4 Microprocessing Systems snd Circuits
No. BP89	Elements of Electronics – Book 5 Communication
No. BP92	Electronics Simplified – Crystal Set Construction
No. BP111	Elements of Electronics – Book 6 Audio

THE PRE-COMPUTER BOOK

by
F. A. Wilson
C.G.I.A., C.Eng., F.I.E.E., F.I.E.R.E., F.B.I.M.

BERNARD BABANI (publishing) LTD
THE GRAMPIANS
SHEPHERDS BUSH ROAD
LONDON W6 7NF
ENGLAND

Although every care has been taken with the preparation of this book, the publishers or author will not be held responsible in any way for any errors that might occur.

© 1983 BERNARD BABANI (publishing) LTD

First Published – April 1983

British Library Cataloguing in Publication Data
Wilson, F. A.
　The pre-computer book. – (BP115)
　1. Microcomputers
　I. Title
　001.64'04　QA76.5

ISBN 0 85934 090 2

Printed and bound in Great Britain by Cox & Wyman Ltd, Reading

PREFACE

When faced with the fact that the upsurge in computers is destined to have more and more effect on our lives, it is obviously desirable that we should at least know something about them, more so if we are likely to possess one or have recently taken the plunge. Even with absolutely no intention of owning one or perhaps almost driven to distraction with hearing about them, the need to be a little informed remains. Moreover young people with an early interest may find that it develops into a career with greatly enhanced likelihood of continuous employment. Factories and offices are increasingly using computerised systems so a little computer awareness may be a distinct advantage in impressing a prospective employer.

Written mainly for those who have no computer nor even have been associated with one, this book is not therefore preparation for any particular model. However, because of the popularity of the ZX81, a low-cost personal or home computer especially useful for beginners, there is a bias in that direction.

What we hope to do is to make entry into the computer world with all its mystique and jargon much less painful. Without just a little help the newcomer is bewildered by advertisements and later mystified by the instruction book. There is little doubt that many of the less expensive computers end up back in their packing boxes when the initial enthusiasm for purchase wanes on the feeling that programming is not such a bed of roses after all. Thus here we do not get involved in anything too complicated or technical, our purpose is merely to let a little light in on what makes a computer tick and a program run. Libraries and bookshops are inundated with literature anxious to take us on from there.

Finally, let's be honest, this is not a book for the expert nor for anybody who already programs successfully, it is only for the non-owner or newcomer who has the feeling of being left in the dark.

In some aspects, especially in arithmetic, one must avoid preaching to the converted hence certain principles, elementary to some but long forgotten by others, are moved to appendices.

F. A. Wilson

CONTENTS

	Page
Chapter 1. QUESTION TIME	1
1.1 What is a computer?	1
1.2 What can one do for me?	1
1.3 How can it do so much yet cost so little?	2
1.4 How is it all done?	3
Chapter 2. BINARY AND DIGITAL	4
2.1 Numbering systems	4
2.2 Binary numbers	5
2.3 Computers use binary	7
2.4 Computers are digital	10
Chapter 3. THE BITS AND PIECES	13
3.1 Processors	16
3.2 Keyboards	17
3.3 Video screens	18
3.4 Memory, an introduction	20
Chapter 4. MEMORY IN ACTION	24
4.1 ROM	24
4.2 RAM	25
4.3 Addressing	26
4.4 Character generation	28
4.5 Tape storage	29
Chapter 5. THE COMPUTER IN ACTION	32
5.1 Programming	32
5.2 Machine code programming	33
5.3 High-level languages	33
Chapter 6. CHATTING IT UP	36
6.1 Bugs and syntax	37
6.2 Cursors	37
6.3 The answer back	38
6.4 Printing	38

Chapter 7. THE BARE BONES OF BASIC — SINGLE INSTRUCTIONS 43
7.1 Calculations 43
7.2 Accuracy 44
7.3 Trigonometry 45
7.4 Random numbers 46
7.5 Other functions 47

Chapter 8. THE BARE BONES OF BASIC — PROGRAMS 49
8.1 Variables 50
8.2 Loops 52
8.3 Conditionals 54
8.4 PEEK and POKE 56
8.5 Graphics 57
8.6 Summary 60

Chapter 9. STORING PROGRAMS 61

IN CONCLUSION 64

Appendix 1. EXPONENTS 65
A1.1 Scientific notation 67

Appendix 2. MORE ABOUT BINARY 68
A.2.1 Binary addition 68
A.2.2 Binary permutations 70

Appendix 3. HEXADECIMAL 72

Appendix 4. GRAPH CO-ORDINATES 73

Appendix 5. TABLES 76
A5.1 Table of Decimal, Binary and Hexadecimal Equivalents 76
A5.2 Table of Powers of 2 78

Chapter One

QUESTION TIME

> O! this learning, what a thing it is.
> *The Taming of the Shrew* – William Shakespeare

In this foray into the computing jungle there are obviously some questions we should like answered before really getting going.

1.1 What is a computer?

Computers appear in all shapes and sizes, from a large room full of expensive equipment and flashing lights down to a small, even pocket-sized affair, in the home. Irrespective of size though, the basic principles are similar and a computer is essentially a device which takes in information and *processes* it, for example, to give an answer to a problem, control a robot or play a game. We tell it exactly what to do and it remembers our orders until we wish it to forget. In it we have a participant fantastically quick, hard-working and clever but with an IQ of zero, it cannot *think* for itself. It is friendly and helpful but does not tolerate slackness in others.

1.2 What can one do for me?

Whether we like it or not, for one can have too much of a good thing, we are now entering an era of *information technology*. In this computers play a great part and the resulting transformation of society is quietly but inexorably going on all around us. Computers are prominent in businesses, factories, schools, transport, homes, in fact they are almost everywhere. Is it not to our advantage therefore that we should understand just a little of what it is all about if only to avoid the feeling of being totally inadequate when all others seem to be computer wizards?

In the home a small computer can become a useful and active member of the family. The answer to the question is that it can educate, amuse and frustrate not only the younger children but also big brother or sister and mum and dad. Its significance may be even greater for those thinking about a future career for more and more jobs will demand some acquaintance with computing machines. Why not therefore get the kids going as soon as possible especially as computer technology is already becoming part of school life? But the clever little box of tricks does not stop at education, it can play challenging games, help with the household finance, do all the dull and difficult calculations, draw pictures, plot graphs, switch things on and off and even tell the time. All this from one single small device simply because it is *programmable* but here is the rub, *we* have to do the programming.

In this process we tell the computer what to do by typing instructions on its keyboard. Advertisements glibly announce that children of only a few years do this but there certainly is not such a genius in every home. Nevertheless with patience, dedication and a modicum of dexterity with arithmetic, there is no real obstacle to painless programming. In return there is the fascination of seeing one's plans brought to fruition, a pleasure which for many ultimately becomes an obsession and with entitlement to the label "computer nut". Writing one's own programs however is not essential, they abound in plenty in computer magazines and books, already written, tested and waiting to be typed in. Going one stage further, programs can be bought, for example for educating children, business use or the more complicated games. These are usually "written" on a standard cassette tape and are fed directly into the home computer which is then immediately ready to go.

It all looks so simple, and with some experience it is, especially with the bit of help this book provides.

1.3 How can it do so much yet cost so little?

This is one of the wonders of modern times. Not so many years ago computers contained a multitude of discrete (separate) components, mainly transistors which we know have revolutionized electronics. Each component had two or more terminals and was connected into the electrical *circuit* by wires soldered to them. Later on the wiring was *printed* in copper on a plastic sheet. Thus with many thousands of components and even more soldered connexions together with plugs and sockets so that panels of components could be withdrawn for maintenance, faults and failures were many and comparison of an early computer's down time (out of order) with its up time (working) left much to be desired.

The body of a transistor is tiny, usually smaller than a peanut but the part where all the action takes place is truly minute and it is formed on silicon, one of the non-metallic elements. Eventually therefore the technique was developed of manufacturing many transistors together on one tiny slice or *chip* of silicon in such a way that they were automatically interconnected and very little wiring was necessary, even then this was also provided on the chip. The whole process is a tribute to human ingenuity and the size has now been reduced so much that many tens of thousands of components are contained on one chip of silicon only about 6mm x 6mm (roughly ¼-inch square). Because everything is combined on the one chip it is known as an *integrated circuit* (IC).

To design and produce the first chip or IC costs a fortune. Thereafter each one costs comparatively little (silicon is not expensive) thus commercially IC's are only designed when there is likelihood of use in large quantities. We reap the benefit of this technology in that the very low cost and size of electronic devices is available to all, hence the home computer has arrived.

1.4 How is it all done?

Ah! that is the subject of the rest of the book. We cannot get far without just a little understanding of the basic principles on which computer technology is founded. Thus we start in the next chapter by finding out why a computer is said to be a *binary digital* device.

Chapter Two

BINARY AND DIGITAL

We who have grown up with the apparent simplicity of the decimal (of ten) system may wonder why the method was not developed earlier than it was. The Romans for example, used what would now be considered to be a cumbersome method, expressing the date in their way is proof enough. Other nations developed ways of numbering but none could be credited with so many advantages as are possessed by the decimal method. We have to thank the early Hindus for its invention, although it was introduced to Europe in the 10th century by the Arabs. They now seem to have most of the credit for it is generally referred to as the "Arabic" system.

2.1 Numbering systems

With decimals, each of the numerals used is a single character (compare the Arabic 8 with the Roman VIII) and the Arabic system is based on a superior principle of *place-value*, that is, the value represented by each numeral depends in a systematic way on its position within the number. As an example, the number two hundred and twenty-two is written in figures as 222 but each 2 represents a different value, the right-hand one is in units, i.e. 2, the middle in tens, i.e. 20 and the left-hand in hundreds, i.e. 200, the sum, 200 + 20 + 2. The right-hand digit of a number is said to be the *least significant*, the left-hand digit, *most significant*.

When the system began it had the numerals 1–9 with a special one for 10, the 0 had not arrived. It was thus incomplete in that there was no built-in way of distinguishing between, say, 25 and 205. Then came the 0 or zero, one of the world's great inventions, so perfecting the decimal system and by about the 16th century Roman numerals had completely lost their place in arithmetic.

Summing up the salient points of the decimal system:

(i) it is a place-value system in that each move to the left in a number of more than one numeral increases the value of the figure by 10 times, each move to the right decreases it to one-tenth.
(ii) the number of symbols needed is 10.
(iii) 10 is called the *radix* of the system (from Latin, = root).

A numbering system radix need not be 10. Historically the ancient Babylonians used 60 (think of the multiplication tables!) and a not so ancient Indian people known as the Maya used 20. Nowadays computers use a radix of 2 and the system is known as *binary* [of 2, the decimal system is also known as *denary* (of ten)]. Binary is accordingly a place-value system needing two symbols only. At this stage we take it for granted that there are good reasons for the computer working better with a radix of 2 rather than 10, these will become evident later.

2.2 Binary numbers

The two symbols have to be chosen, the choice is limitless but perhaps the most obvious is 0 and 1, that is by borrowing the first two symbols from the established denary system. So that the symbol 0 does not get mixed up with the letter O, computer people usually write the 0 with an oblique stroke, thus ∅, but it means exactly the same as 0. Because we ourselves intend to join the computing intelligentsia we too will use ∅.

So far we have decimal 0 = binary ∅ (or 0) and decimal 1 = binary 1, no problem. What about decimal 2? (Note the use of the term "decimal" instead of "denary", it is more common.) Remember the place-value rule — for each move to the left the symbol value is multiplied by the radix, therefore a binary 1 in the second place (moving right to left) has a decimal value of 2 and in the third place of 4, i.e.

decimal 2 = binary 1∅   [(1 × 2) + (∅ × 1)]

decimal 3 = binary 11   [(1 × 2) + (1 × 1)]

where in each of the smaller brackets the second figure represents the place value. Note that when anything is multiplied by zero (∅), the result is zero, hence (∅ × 1) = ∅.

There are only two symbols to play with. Therefore, for decimal 4 three binary figures are required, i.e.

decimal 4 = binary 1∅∅   [(1 × 4) + (∅ × 2) + (∅ × 1)]

and

decimal 5 = binary 1∅1   [(1 × 4) + (∅ × 2) + (1 × 1)]

decimal 6 = binary 11∅   [(1 × 4) + (1 × 2) + (∅ × 1)]

decimal 7 = binary 111   [(1 × 4) + (1 × 2) + (1 × 1)]

and to continue further four binary figures are needed.

Generally the decimal equivalent of a binary number can be found by writing the latter in a row of boxes as shown in Fig. 2.1(i) then adding all the box results together. Thus binary 1∅∅∅ = decimal [(1 × 8) + (∅ × 4) + (∅ × 2) + (∅ × 1)] = 8 and binary 11∅∅∅11 = decimal [(1 × 64) + (1 × 32) + (∅ × 16) + (∅ × 8) + (∅ × 4) + (1 × 2) + (1 × 1)] = 99.

In reverse, to find the binary equivalent of a decimal number we clearly must be able first to find the largest box number which applies. Take 99 as the example. The most significant binary digit must be equivalent to 64 (128 is too large) so a 1 is put in the 64 box (and a ∅ in the 128 box for completeness) as shown in Fig. 2.1(ii). Subtracting 64 from 99 leaves 35. Next 32 can be taken out of this, leaving 3 so a 1 goes into the 32 box. 16, 8 and 4 cannot be taken from 3 so these boxes get zeros. 3 we already known is binary 11, i.e. 1 in the 2-box, 1 in the 1-box, thus decimal 99 = binary ∅11∅∅∅11. Note that zeroes on the left of the binary number, unlike zeros within the number, have no effect, they are simply used when required to tidy things up.

Computing is not without its own shorthand, so we normally write $99_{10} = \emptyset 11\emptyset\emptyset 11_2$, the little figure at the bottom indicating the radix.

At this point we begin to make use of the Appendices. Appendix 1 is useful if some of our arithmetic is a little

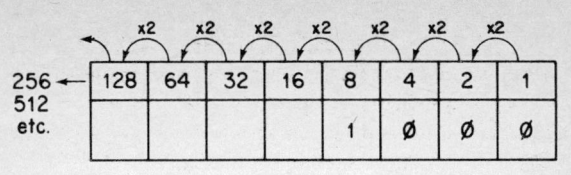

	128	64	32	16	8	4	2	1
256 ← 512 etc.								
					1	Ø	Ø	Ø

(×2 between each column)

(i) binary 1ØØØ = decimal 8

128	64	32	16	8	4	2	1
Ø	1	1	Ø	Ø	Ø	1	1

(ii) decimal 99 = binary Ø11ØØØ11

2^7	2^6	2^5	2^4	2^3	2^2	2^1	2^0
Ø	1	1	Ø	Ø	Ø	1	1

(iii) figure (ii) redrawn with column headings expressed as powers of 2

Fig. 2.1 Decimal/binary equivalents

rusty so it ensures that we understand the headings of the table of Fig. 2.1(iii) while Appendix 2 provides a little more general help with binary notation.

So far then we are convinced that in place-value numbering systems a radix of any *integer* (whole number) can be used. It must be an integer because the number of symbols is equal to the radix and there cannot be a fraction of a symbol. It is also evident that by labelling the value of each place as in Fig. 2.1, change from one radix to another is straightforward. No worries here though, although we are decimal and the computer binary, it makes the changes for us.

2.3 Computers use binary

What is most striking from Fig. 2.1 is that binary numbers greater than 1 all have more figures or *digits* than their decimal equivalents, seemingly a disadvantage because operations such as addition, multiplication, etc. need many more steps. This is more than compensated for by the fact that each binary step is much simpler and in a computer over one million single steps (such as adding or multiplying a ∅ and a 1) can be accomplished within one second, thus two 8-figure decimal numbers can be multiplied or divided in about one-tenth of a second. We with decimals are still at the starting post when the computer with its binary has finished.

We may be assured that computers use binary *notation* (a set of symbols) but we have yet to be convinced that a radix as low as 2 is necessary, why not a higher value or why not stay with 10 and avoid all the problems of conversion? To talk in a book on computers about the defeat of the Spanish Armada in 1588 may seem ludicrous in the extreme. Nevertheless if we let our imaginations run riot it can in a simple way provide the starting point needed. Information that the Armada was sailing up the English Channel was carried from hilltop to hilltop by bonfires. This might be considered as a binary system for there were two symbols or states only:

no bonfire (∅) meaning "nothing in sight", or

bonfire (1) meaning "the Armada is on its way".

But just suppose the designer of the system was charged with also communicating whether there were less or more than, say, 50 ships. What might spring to mind could be:

no bonfire (∅)   — nothing in sight

small bonfire (1) — coming with 50 or less ships

large bonfire (2) — coming with more than 50 ships,

a *ternary* (of three) system because there are three different symbols.

The possibility of error is immediately obvious. Unlike the certainty of being able to distinguish between no bonfire and a bonfire even though many miles away, trying to determine whether a bonfire is large or small may be fraught with difficulty, especially when there is a mist or the observer is short-sighted. The designer would truly have lost all prospects of promotion and perhaps even his head if the wrong information got through.

Now let him try again with a binary system:

    no bonfire (∅)   – nothing in sight

    one bonfire (1)   – coming with 50 or less ships

    two bonfires (2)   – coming with more than 50 ships,

binary because there are only two different symbols and distinguishing between them is easy. Short of thick fog, the likelihood of error is now practically zero.

This is also the story of the computer. It receives its instructions and carries out its work by sensing the presence or absence not of bonfires but of electrical *voltages*, usually about 5 volts which is approximately that of a 3-cell torch battery. No voltage = binary ∅, 5 volts = binary 1. If, on the other hand, the computer were to work decimally, then there would be a range of ten different voltages each of which must be received and measured correctly. The method can work but as shown for the Armada, with high risk of error because in the practical world so many things arise to shift a voltage from its intended value.

Thus binary is the internal language of the computer, numbers are held and manipulated as we have seen in a binary *code*. In a computer binary instructions and data are said to be in *machine language*. It is truly amazing how many millions of operations are carried out without a single error. This has to be because in all arithmetical work errors are disastrous — think of £89 (binary 1∅11∅∅1) paid into a computerized bank account. If the first binary 1 were to be misread as a ∅, the amount credited would be ∅∅11∅∅1, £64 short!

2.4 Computers are digital

Generally information can be carried electronically in two different fashions, *analogue* or *digital*. We can perhaps get an inkling of the difference by considering the two types of watch, the analogue one with hands going round and telling the time all the time and alternatively the digital type which indicates the time not by a moving pointer but by a periodic display of numbers. In the latter case the time is not shown continuously but at intervals.

A useful thought only, not an explanation but one follows for we do need some idea of this particular feature of the computer because it helps to clarify many other explanations to come.

Fig. 2.2(i) shows a simple electronic circuit as used in an electric handlamp, it comprises a source of electricity, in this case a battery, a switch and a lamp. When the arm of the switch is up nothing happens, the battery is unable to drive a *current* round the circuit because one wire is "broken" at the switch. When the switch is operated (as shown dotted) the metallic circuit is completed and electric current flows from one terminal of the battery, through the filament of the lamp and back to the other battery terminal. The battery voltage (i.e. its electrical pressure or driving force, in this case 3 or 4.5 volts) controls the amount of electric current going round and is such that the lamp lights correctly, too much current burns out the lamp filament, too little produces insufficient light.

Suppose we use such a device for communicating, say simply the number 9 to an observer some distance away. (Morse code using an Aldis lamp has some similarities but it is a comparatively slow system.) Binary 9 is 1∅∅1 and if the switch is off for a ∅ and on for a 1 we might think we are home and dry but we are not, there are two problems:

(i) Can the observer be sure that there are two ∅'s, not one or three?
(ii) Considering that binary numbers have different numbers of digits, how does the observer know when one

(i) simple electronic circuit

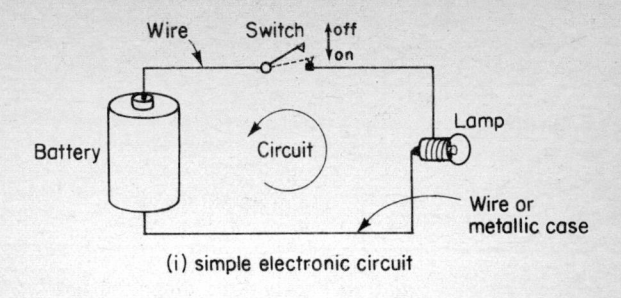

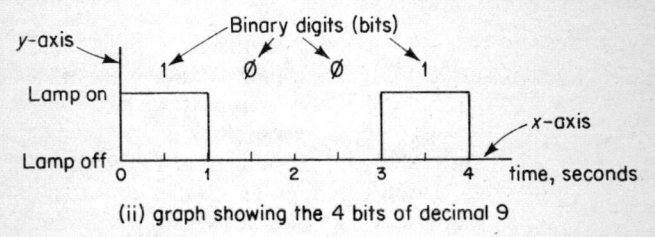

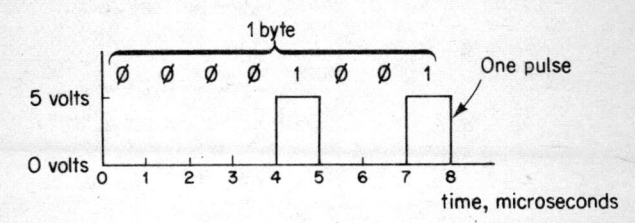

(ii) graph showing the 4 bits of decimal 9

(iii) as (ii) but in computer form

Fig. 2.2 Digital transmission

number has been completed and the next is beginning?

The first difficulty is overcome by both the sender and the observer working strictly to time, say, transmitting one *bi*nary dig*it* (known in the digital world as a *bit*) every second. With watches synchronized, for decimal 9 the observer would see a light during the first second, none in seconds 2 and 3 and again a light in the 4th. For human beings, working at this speed which is one *bit per second* (b/s) is possible but at

11

10 b/s not. For digital systems (such as the computer) such speeds are undemanding, they can shift *millions* of bits from one place to another in a single second.

To refresh our memories about graphs (and we ought to be conversant with them for programming later so there is a little help in Appendix 4) this feature is illustrated in Fig. 2.2(ii). The x-axis (i.e. the horizontal one) is marked in intervals of time and on the y-axis the two states of the lamp are indicated, simply on or off and theoretically changing over in no time. From 0 to 1 second the lamp is on, indicating a binary 1, between 1 and 2, and also between 2 and 3 seconds it is off for ØØ and finally on from 3 to 4 seconds for another 1.

The second difficulty of knowing when a number has been completed is overcome by always transmitting a fixed number or block of bits. A commonly used block is 8 and with this decimal 9 becomes ØØØØ1ØØ1, seemingly a wasteful method but essential in the well organized electronics of computers. Because a block of 8 bits is so frequently used it has a special name, a *byte*, so here is something important to remember:

8 bits make 1 byte.

Rather amusingly, 4 bits make a *nibble*, although this unit is hardly ever used.

Fig. 2.2(iii) shows the graph from (ii) in computer form. For convenience the time units shown are microseconds (μs), i.e. millionths of one second, but in fact they are likely to be even less. As human beings we cannot come to grips with such infinitesimally small times but are grateful for them as one of the secrets of success of the computer.

Switching the lamp on and off to convey information in the shape of the number 9 in the example, is purely for illustration. However within the computer things are not all that different from Fig. 2.2(i). The battery is replaced by a power supply of some 5 or more volts derived from the public supply mains, the switch by a transistor capable of switching on and off at fantastically fast rates and the *bit stream* (the train of pulses at 5 volts for 1 and 0 volts for Ø) does not of course flash a lamp, it operates many other devices to be described later.

Chapter Three

THE BITS AND PIECES

It is a simple fact that a computer can do only what its programmer, given the time and inclination, can do. That the computer does it in a tiny fraction of the time is justification for its existence. In a way therefore the computer is an extension of our inner selves, having been developed to do the more tedious brain work for us. The anatomy of our helpful friend can therefore perhaps be understood better by looking at our own personal functions simultaneously.

We each have a brain, an organ both miraculous and mysterious. It is our powerful centre of sensation and thought, yet as if to bring us down to earth, somewhat resembling a cauliflower. Even if we have yet to find out how it works, we do already have some idea of its organization. It is fed with information from our *sensors* (eyes, ears, tongue, fingers, etc.), even, some would claim, directly from the supernatural. Given this continuous input of information, the brain stores it in the memory, most to be kept for a short term (sometimes too short) but some for longer. If necessary we think about it, do calculations, come to conclusions and make decisions. In so doing we are *processing* the information with the memory backing us as to how we have reacted to similar circumstances in the past or supplying numerical data such as multiplication tables, etc., hammered in while we were at school. The results of such pondering are also stored for immediate or later action. At this more memory is brought into use for the brain has to remember which strings to pull when for example we talk, walk or even sleep. Here we put this all into neat little boxes as in Fig. 3.1(i) in which the arrows on the lines joining the boxes indicate in which direction the information flows. Note also that the brain has to remember *where* to find what is required in the memory.

Comparison of (i) and (ii) in Fig. 3.1 shows how similar is the organization of the computer. It has both short- and

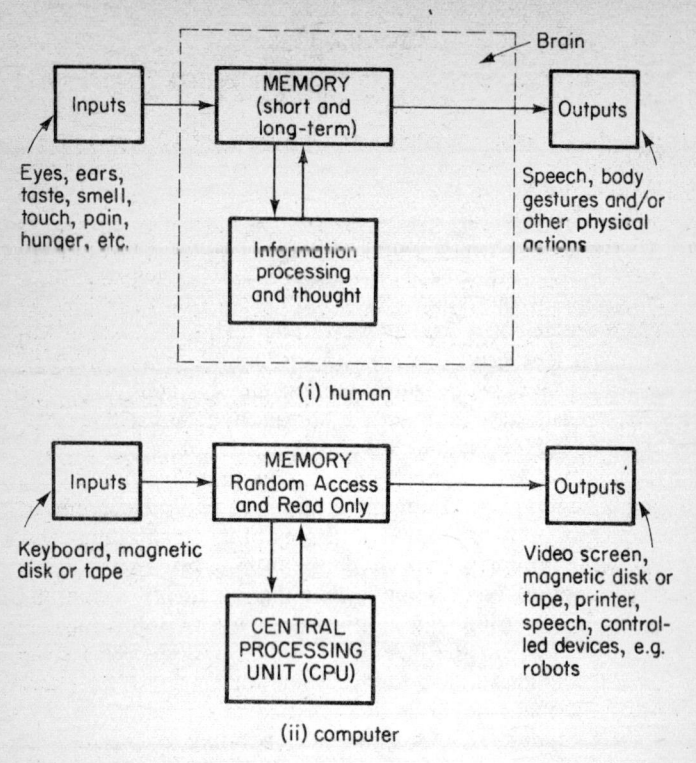

```
                                                          Brain
         ┌─────────┐     ┌──────────────┐        ┌─────────┐
         │ Inputs  │────▶│   MEMORY     │───────▶│ Outputs │
         └─────────┘     │ (short and   │        └─────────┘
                         │  long-term)  │
Eyes, ears,              └──────┬───────┘         Speech, body
taste, smell,                   │  ▲              gestures and/or
touch, pain,                    ▼  │              other physical
hunger, etc.             ┌──────────────┐         actions
                         │ Information  │
                         │ processing   │
                         │ and thought  │
                         └──────────────┘
```

(i) human

```
         ┌─────────┐     ┌──────────────┐        ┌─────────┐
         │ Inputs  │────▶│   MEMORY     │───────▶│ Outputs │
         └─────────┘     │Random Access │        └─────────┘
                         │and Read Only │
Keyboard, magnetic       └──────┬───────┘         Video screen,
disk or tape                    │  ▲              magnetic disk or
                                ▼  │              tape, printer,
                         ┌──────────────┐         speech, control-
                         │   CENTRAL    │         led devices, e.g.
                         │  PROCESSING  │         robots
                         │  UNIT (CPU)  │
                         └──────────────┘
```

(ii) computer

Fig. 3.1 Memory and processing arrangements

long-term memories but with different titles which we will understand later. Memory is important to computer users because it has a frustrating habit of running out. When it does so there is no hope of stuffing in more information as is done with our own memories, the computer will not accept a single extra byte because it cannot. Memory is a facility which can be purchased separately and because of its importance we will look at it in more detail later. Fortunately although human memory is capricious, the computer's is not. The computer also has a processor (CPU) taking information from the memory and returning it duly manipulated. The word "thought" does not appear in the box for as we now appreciate, the computer is not a thinking device. Of the inputs and outputs shown, those met in the home first are the keyboard on which the instructions and input data are typed and a television-type screen (or in many cases an actual television receiver) on which the computer displays the output. Pocket computers however, manage without a full screen and use a display instead which prints a single line only. They tend to resemble overgrown calculators yet have at their command almost as much computing power as have their bigger brothers. Magnetic tape cassettes may also be used for both input and output while some owners find living unbearable without a printer, a device which records on paper what is seen on the screen. The keyboard, screen and other items appropriate to the input and output boxes are known as *peripherals* (on the boundary). The general arrangement is shown in Fig. 3.2 and although pictured separately any two or even all three of the units may be combined. A combination of keyboard and video screen is known as a *visual display unit* (VDU)

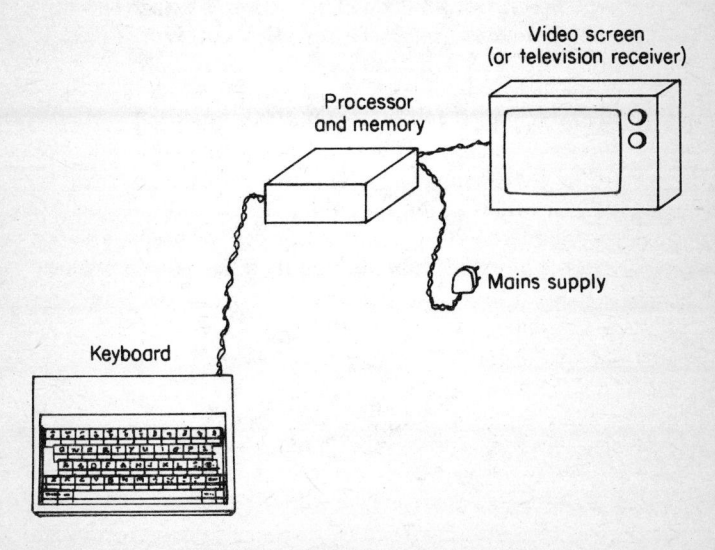

Fig. 3.2 Main units of a computer

3.1 Processors

Of all the units of a computer, this one works hardest. It constantly checks the keyboard to see when a key is depressed, monitors and updates the display on the screen and accepts and carries out all our instructions provided that they are presented to it in binary form. This could be done directly by the programmer but he or she needs to be expert and dedicated for success. With most computers and practically all personal ones there is less wear and tear on the user's nerves because the computer embodies a special program which takes instructions more suited to us ordinary humans. These instructions are in a form near enough to everyday language to be easily understood and the program converts them into binary for us. This program is hidden away in the computer memory and is a subject to be considered later when we devote ourselves to programming.

As might be gathered from Chapter One the processor or *Central Processing Unit* (CPU) is mostly within a single integrated circuit (on a silicon chip). Its size is such that the term *microprocessor* (micro is from Greek *mikros*, small) is appropriate and a sketch of a typical one is given in Fig. 3.3. It contains many thousands of transistor-type devices. The silicon chip occupies a small area in the centre of the device with wires emanating from it to the connecting pins along the edge, 40 or more altogether. This number of connexions to the outside world is an indication of the electronic complexity of computing but this need not worry us, nor need we know how a microprocessor carries out all its tasks with such speed

Fig. 3.3 A microprocessor

and precision, we have enough on our plates in simply drawing up a rough sketch of the whole process. A computer based on a microprocessor is often referred to as a *microcomputer*.

3.2 Keyboards

Most, but not all, follow closely the standard typewriter keyboard layout, the top row of alphabetical keys running QWERTY etc. Typing is fun for most people and it is best when starting from scratch to use all the fingers of both hands, imagining a line splitting the keyboard into left and right halves and using the appropriate hand to suit. Action is smoother and eventually quicker than with one or two index fingers only. Keyboards of the touch type (i.e. the key is not depressed, the finger merely touches a painted rectangle) do not lend themselves to fast typing in this way. Pictures of computer keyboards in advertisements may show not only the standard keys (as in Fig. 3.2) but in addition a block of 16 to the right. On some keyboards, usually on the more expensive machines, these extra keys are *hexadecimal*, they ease the burden of entering instructions in binary and we look at their use in Chapter Five.

So far we have discussed binary numbers and the fact that the processor in manipulating them has to be switched into the appropriate actions by *binary instructions*, that is, a series of Ø's and 1's which switch on or off the appropriate electronic circuits as required. These binary instructions therefore have no numerical meaning although each must have a binary number equivalent. It just so happens that the same electrical pulses which convey binary numbers are also usable for turning tiny electronic switches on and off. As a single example the byte ØØØØ11Ø1 received by the processor while awaiting instructions as to what action to take might tell it to switch its circuits ready for addition. Subsequently when adding numbers the same byte would indicate the decimal number 13.

Binary digits now have a further job to do which is to represent the letters of the alphabet, punctuation marks and all the other symbols used. Fortunately a standard code for these has been adopted to which nearly all keyboards conform, it is called the *ASCII Code* which is shorthand for the "American Standard Code for Information Interchange". All ASCII characters use a 7-bit code for 128 different combinations, (see Appendix A2.2), made up to 1 byte with a spare bit which is conveniently used for checking purposes. As an example, the capital letters of the alphabet might use binary codes which happen to be numbers having decimal equivalents 65–90 thus:

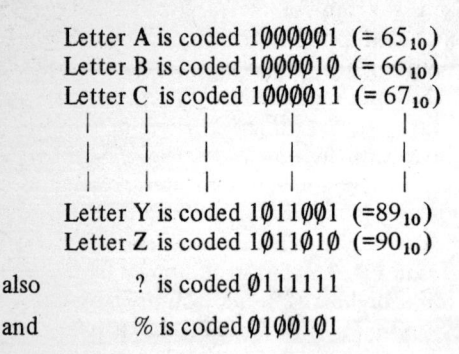

>   Letter A is coded 1000001 (= 65_{10})
>   Letter B is coded 1000010 (= 66_{10})
>   Letter C is coded 1000011 (= 67_{10})
> | | | | |
> | | | | |
> | | | | |
>   Letter Y is coded 1011001 (= 89_{10})
>   Letter Z is coded 1011010 (= 90_{10})

also   ? is coded 0111111

and   % is coded 0100101

(back to Sect. 2.2 for the method of checking the equivalence of binary and decimal numbers or to the Table in Appendix A5.1 for the easy way out).

It may seem odd perhaps but there are operational reasons for the numerals 0–9 having codes instead of their correct binary numbers. There is also no gain in our quoting all the ASCII Codes, all we need to know is that when a key is depressed the appropriate binary code is generated by the keyboard, made up to 1 byte and transmitted to the memory.

3.3 Video screens

Just as there are about 40 lines of print on this page and some 60 characters (letters, numbers, symbols, spaces) per line, so a computer writes a fixed number of lines on a video display screen with a certain number of characters per line. The range of characters per line for various computers is from about 30 to 80, usually 30–40 with from 16 up to about 50 lines, 25 being commonly used. The *resolution* which might loosely be defined as the "sharpness" of the image varies with the model and as with a television (tv) picture, the distance from which the screen is viewed is important. Note that "lines" here are not the same as the normal tv picture lines which are mostly 625 or 525.

Normally a computer generates *video* (Latin, I see) electronic signals which pass directly to its monitor or video screen as shown in Fig. 3.4(i). The job of the complete monitor is to write the words on the screen as represented

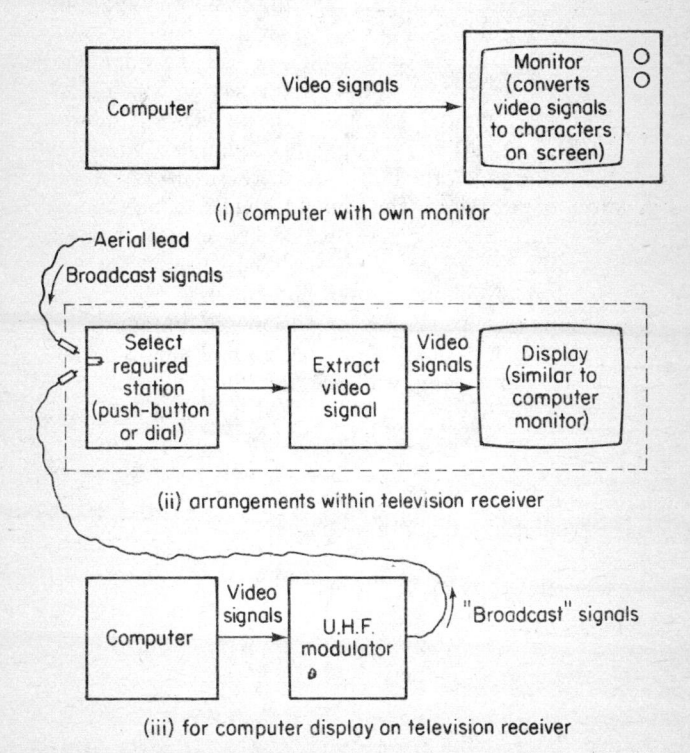

(i) computer with own monitor

(ii) arrangements within television receiver

(iii) for computer display on television receiver

Fig. 3.4 Visual display

by the video signals. Many home computers however keep the price low by making use of a standard tv set in place of a monitor. Although from the user's point of view the system should be simple to connect up and use, it may be helpful to understand a little of how it works.

Television video signals cannot be broadcast directly but are "carried" by another type of signal which can. This *carrier* is known as a uhf one (ultra high frequency). Each separate transmission has a *channel* number and it is "tuned in" on a tv set either by rotating a station selector dial or via an already tuned push button in the same way as we select medium- and long-wave stations on a transistor radio set. A tv set is therefore more complicated than a monitor because in addition it has first to select the required tv station from the several offered to it by the aerial and then extract the video signal. The latter is then passed to the display section which closely resembles the computer monitor. The sequence is shown in Fig. 3.4(ii). At (iii) is the additional equipment known as a *uhf modulator* which the computer therefore needs for working into a tv receiver. The computer video signals are first impressed on a uhf carrier (as would happen in a tv broadcasting station) working on a specified channel (or wavelength) which is chosen so as not to clash with normal transmissions (e.g. in the UK on Channel 36 on which no tv station operates). Thus the normal tv aerial plug is removed from the set and replaced with one from the computer and the tv set is tuned to the channel quoted by the manufacturer (e.g. 36). If the set is a push-button type, one spare button is specially tuned. The connexions are simple although comparing (iii) and (ii) in the Figure with (i) shows just how complicated electronically things have become. Perhaps the greatest complication though is in deciding who uses the family television set.

3.4 Memory, an introduction

Unlike human memory which always plays tricks, that in a computer is precise, what is more it never forgets unless made to and it then does this completely, nothing lingers. Computer memories are integrated circuits and consist of thousands of electronic "cells" in each of which a $\emptyset$ or a 1 can be "stored" and as often as is required the cell can be "read" to see which it is. Before looking in more detail at these points however we ought to clear the air about the mysterious K which seems to crop up whenever computers are discussed. K is a letter which has been steadily creeping into our lives with metrication. Short for *kilo*, it came originally from the Greek, meaning one thousand. The metric k is a small one and it still stands for 1000, no more, no less. Thus a kilogramme (kg) is 1000 grammes, a kilometre (km) 1000 metres. Computers on the other hand are not metric so their K is different, it is a capital one and as if to deliberately confuse us, stands for 2^{10} or 1024 (Appendix A5.2). Accordingly a *kilobit* means 1024 bits and a *kilobyte* means 1024 bytes, eight times as much. Usually the capacity of a block of memory is quoted as say, 1 K, 16K etc. in which cases the K refers to kilobytes, a 16K memory therefore can store 16 x 1024 bytes, i.e. it has 16 x 1024 x 8 individual memory cells.

Larger capacities still are rated in *megabits* or more usually, *megabytes*. Mega is from the Greek for "great" which in metrication means 1,000,000, but for computers 2^{20}, i.e. 1,048,576 so a memory capacity quoted as 1M usually indicates 1,048,576 *bytes*. Clearly whether the K and M refer to bits or bytes should always be stated but in our casual way this is often omitted, and as indicated above the reference is normally to bytes. A memory capacity in the M class does not enter the home, it is too much, more likely capacities are 1K up to 48K.

Let us first consider a single memory cell, it is an electronic circuit which can be set to a $\emptyset$ or a 1 but to nothing else. Electrically this means that if the cell output voltage is measured with an ordinary voltmeter, if set to $\emptyset$ the reading is 0 volts, when set to 1 it is 5V, rather like the difference between a flat and a live torch battery. There are variations on these figures but they are unimportant here. So that the cell cannot be set anywhere in between, it operates with a *toggle* action which is best illustrated by the ordinary home electric light switch. If the lever is moved slowly nothing happens within the switch until it reaches a position where the mechanism takes over, the lever then flies to the opposite rest position and the switch changes over rapidly, it cannot stay half-way. Because of their toggle or somersault action, computer memory circuits have become known as *flip-flops*. In one *millionth* of a second a flip-flop can switch back and forth several times.

The standard unit of memory is not the single cell but eight, thus storing a byte rather than a bit. Consider first 8 electric light switches in a row as sketched in Fig. 3.5(i), some are switched to "on", others remain "off", the whole 8 representing for example, the binary number 11Ø Ø1Ø1Ø (= 202_{10}). The switches could control lamps but we gain little from this because we can see from the switches themselves what the indication is. In computer memory all cells are cleared by restoring them to Ø, the technique is simulated in Fig. 3.5(i) by a rod beneath the switch levers which is raised

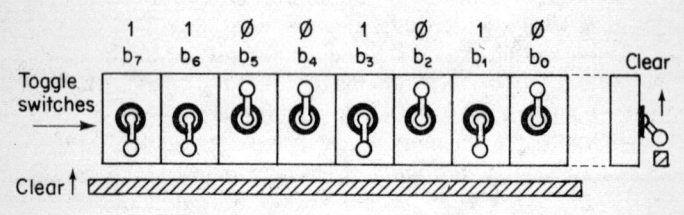

(i) representation of one byte of memory

(ii) small block of memory

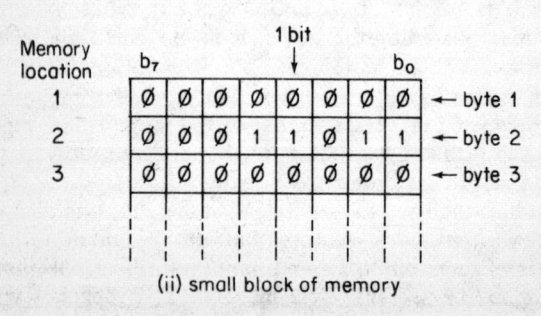

Fig. 3.5 Computer memory

to restore all levers to "off", then lowered again. Subsequently when a binary number or code is written in, 1's operate the switches, ∅'s in fact do nothing.

With this picture in mind we might draw a small block of memory as in Fig. 3.5(ii) where each square represents storage capacity for 1 bit, bytes 1 and 3 are clear and byte 2 stores the decimal number 27. Now squirrels sometimes cannot find the nuts they have stored and to avoid our having the same problem each byte is identified by a numbered address, just like houses in a street. If the address number were contained in 1 byte, only 256 different ones could be catered for (see Appendices A2.2 and A5.2 – 2^8 = 256) therefore most microcomputers use two bytes thus allowing for 2^{16} different addresses, i.e. 65,536 or 64K. This is therefore the maximum number of memory locations which they can use but is usually more than ample and in fact many of the addresses may not be used. We will understand the addressing arrangements better as we progress.

Chapter Four

MEMORY IN ACTION

Although memory comes in many sizes it also comes in several different types, the two most likely to be met first in instruction books or advertisements are *ROM* and *RAM*, briefly described as permanent and not so permanent. Apart from this difference they both have the general features outlined in Chapter Three, that is, they can be considered as in Fig. 3.5(ii), each memory location a byte with an address number somewhere from ∅ to 65,535.

4.1 ROM

The letters stand for *Read-Only Memory*, and it is just that, a memory which is set during manufacture and the information it provides is there for good. We cannot write into it but each location can be read as often as is required. It is the internal memory of the machine and is read by the processor to find out what to do and how to do it for a host of different jobs, for example, reading the various binary instructions which are required each time a character is typed on the keyboard or displayed on the screen.

Another simple example of the use of the ROM is given by the need to have the value of π available (3.1415927, the ratio of the circumference to the diameter of a circle). This could be generated each time by an appropriate program but because it may be called for quite frequently, the value is more likely to be stored permanently in the ROM, thus by knowing the addresses (plural because this particular number occupies more than one byte), the processor can have it on demand.

Within the ROM is also stored the internal program which enables us to talk to the computer more or less in our own language without having to bother with machine language. Altogether so much internal work goes on that a home computer ROM is likely to be of capacity 8K up to, say, 16K or more. 8K infers 8192 bytes, one may wonder just what is required to fill such a larger number of locations especially when we learn that ROM programs are written by people who are expert in saving memory. It demonstrates however just how much goes on inside when the computer is active.

Although we do not use the ROM directly because the processor uses it for us, it will be found later that it is possible to display on the screen what is stored in it by simply telling the computer which memory locations are of interest.

Just in case the initials ROM appear expanded as PROM or EPROM, the first is one which can be programmed by special processing after manufacture and is a *Programmable Read-Only Memory*, while the additional E in the second case stands for *Erasable*, indicating that the ROM can be erased as a whole then completely reprogrammed. We are unlikely to be concerned with either of these but at least now know what the letters stand for.

4.2 RAM

With this type, information can be stored and retrieved at will, it is a "write/read" memory. This is the one which takes in what is typed on the keyboard so storing the programs and data. It must be of sufficient capacity to allow storage of a long program of instructions so that complete jobs can be carried out in one go rather than piecemeal. The letters stand for *Random Access Memory* implying that memory locations are chosen at random, that is, any one location is as likely to be used as any other. This is not strictly true but the term has helped in the past to distinguish it from other types of memory and has stayed with us.

From the reminder in the first paragraph of this chapter, that 64K is the total memory which can be addressed and considering the ROM to require a maximum of, say, 16K address numbers, then the maximum RAM likely to be available is some 48K (in reality slightly less because the processor may need some as "working memory"). In view of the fact that some home computers start the user off with a mere 1K,

48K seems a lot and it is, until one is really hooked. Fortunately memory can usually be added by plugging in extra units.

Now for the snag. With most current RAM's, the contents are lost (i.e. all memory cells return to ∅) if the power to the computer is switched off, most inconvenient when a long program has been typed in and is still wanted. In such circumstances other types of memory such as cassette tape may be called in to take over, this is considered in Chapter Nine. Such RAM's are classed as *volatile* and needless to say, the development of non-volatile memory is proceeding apace.

4.3 Addressing

This is rather like having a safe deposit box in a bank, the right key must be used to get at the contents. Let us design our own key and lock as in Fig. 4.1(i), but although aiming to illustrate a 16-lever system, to avoid repetition in the drawing we use only 4. Hopefully the drawing is self-exlanatory but briefly, projections on the keys (representing 1's) depress the pivotted catches so that the spring is able to move the bar to the right and unlock. Each lock differs according to the binary code and evidently only the correct key can release it, the projections on the key in the wrong positions prevent the key being turned and ∅'s in the wrong positions fail to depress the latches. The Figure is the mechanical analogy of the addressing system of a computer. In this case there are 16 bits instead of 4 and each memory location has an electronic "lock" designed to operate only when the correct 16-bit code is received. These 16 bits of the address code are all applied at the same time from 16 wires known as the *address bus*. (A more descriptive word than bus might be "highway".)

Thus by using the address bus, the one and only memory location in the range ∅ to 65535 is opened up. A second bus or highway is now required to carry data into the memory location when writing or to accept data when reading. This is known as the *data bus* and because computers move 1 byte at a time, the data bus has 8 wires (16 or even 32 in more advanced machines). We now begin to understand why there

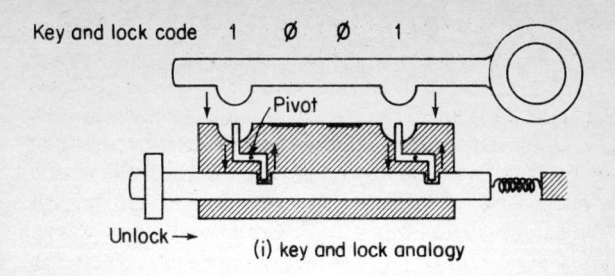

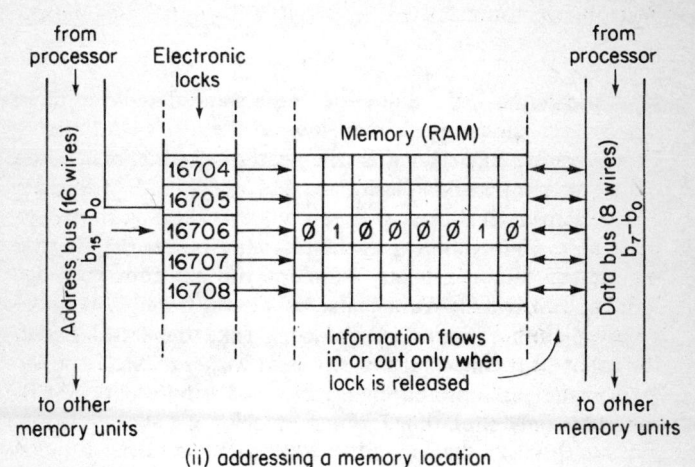

Fig. 4.1 Addressing memory

are so many connexions to a microprocessor (Fig. 3.3), the address and data buses alone account for 24. The system operates basically as in Fig. 4.1(ii). As an example, suppose that the letter B (Section 3.2) is stored in memory location 16706. The processor gains access to this information by first placing the appropriate bits [Ø1ØØØØØ1Ø1ØØØØ1Ø (= 16706_{10})] on the address bus whereupon this location only is unlocked and its contents [Ø1ØØØØ1Ø (= B)] are placed on the data bus for transmission back to the processor. In the other direction the processor writes in the memory by unlocking the location chosen and placing the data bits on the data bus whereupon any data already existing in the memory location is automatically first erased. Note that although the information on the data bus is connected to all memory locations, only the unlocked one can receive it. Also in this particular case the processor must know that ØlØØØØlØ represents the letter B, not the number 66 nor a set of instructions. This is all arranged by the sequence in which the information is provided.

4.4 Character generation

Understanding a little about the address and data buses now allows us to digress for a brief look at the display technique and its use of ROM for this will greatly help in appreciation of basic computer principles.

The screen characters themselves are tucked away in the ROM in a section known as the *character generator*. Things here are of course in binary form and this has nothing to do with the ASCII code for a character, what is stored is in fact a binary picture rather than a code. Take the letter E for example and assume that the processor wishes to write one on the screen. Each stored character needs 8 bytes (its ASCII Code uses only one), thus forming a block 8 x 8 as sketched in Fig. 4.2(i) where the bits are shown stored as for E. Typical memory addresses are also shown. In this example therefore the processor gains access to letter E by placing the binary codes for 8016 − 8023 in succession on the address bus, this it does through a simple built-in program of its own. Accordingly the appropriate bytes appear one after the other on the data bus.

A tv picture or computer monitor screen is illuminated by a tiny spot of light which traverses as indicated in Fig. 4.2(ii). The spot moves from left to right across the screen, quickly returning to the left each time (the *flyback*) and moving down from the top so that the whole screen is covered. This happens 50 times in one second (60 in USA). If the spot is bright all the time then we see a blank (illuminated) screen. Next suppose that the processor uses the binary codes from the character generator so that the ∅'s leave the spot bright but 1's black it out and it does this for one byte on each traverse of the spot commencing at the same distance across the screen. Fig. 4.2(iii) suggests that we can consider the moving spot as a series of white or black dots printed on the screen, repeated 50 times a second to give us the impression of a continuous, stationary picture. Referring back to the binary code pattern for letter E as shown in (i) it is now easy to see how it is transferred to the screen and printed. A slightly simplified explanation but from it and what has gone before we can now imagine what happens when a key is pressed and the computer is asked to display the character on the screen:

(i) on depressing the key the ASCII code for the character is placed in one byte of the memory (RAM);
(ii) the processor reads this and looks up the address of the first byte in the character generator (ROM);
(iii) this byte and the following 7 are read out and transmitted to the monitor in a form suitable for printing the character.

4.5 Tape storage

This as far as we are concerned means using magnetic cassette tape as external memory. ∅'s and 1's can be recorded along a tape as short bursts of low and high tones. We have already discovered that switching off most computers creates a lapse of memory, the loss can be avoided however by shifting the data first onto a cassette tape residing in an everyday home tape recorder and it need not be an expensive one. The more expensive computers have their own cassette recorders built in.

The data is recorded on the tape *serially* (one byte after the other) and is much less accessible. The big boys use disks with moving pick-up heads so that they can get to any part of the recording quickly but this facility is expensive and therefore not generally used with personal computers. To use a stored program it must first be played back into the computer

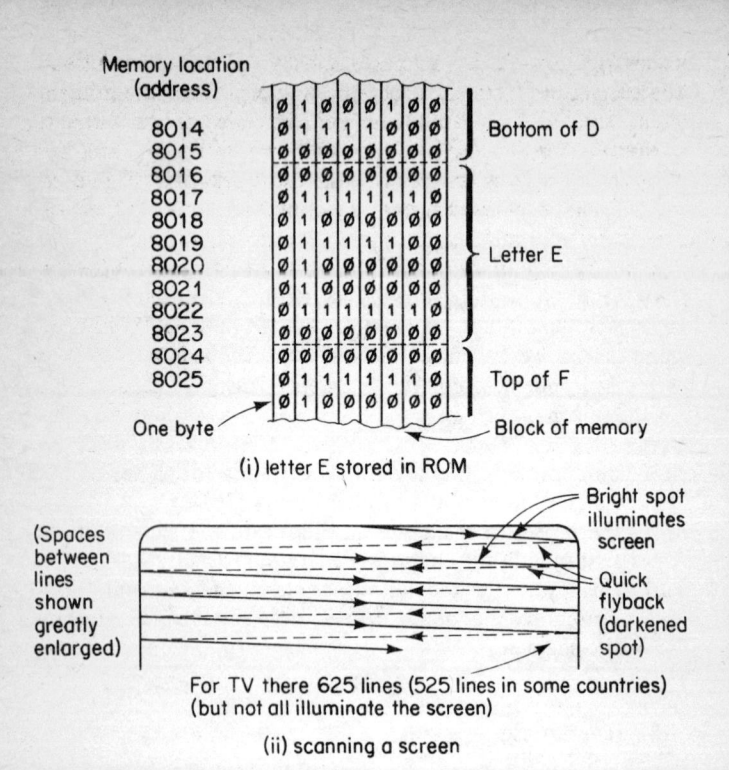

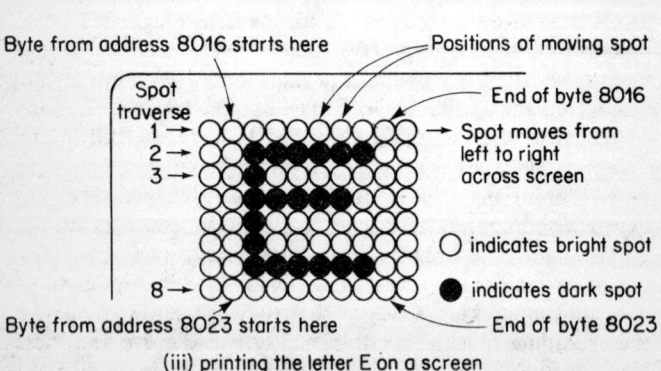

Fig. 4.2 Character generation

memory where in fact it was originally. The technique has another worth-while advantage, programs can be bought already recorded on tape, these are fed in and at a stroke the computer is programmed, this can be repeated any number of times. Programs are known as *software* which distinguishes them from the *hardware* which is a general term for the bits and pieces we can drop or trip over.

We will look at the practicalities of tape storage in Chapter 9.

Chapter Five

THE COMPUTER IN ACTION

We now know a little about *how* a computer works but hereon the tussle begins for *when* it works we have to pull the strings. Like so many jobs in which practice makes perfect, programming also demands devotion and patience. Accordingly we move forward slowly for a full understanding of what each step is trying to achieve is indispensable.

5.1 Programming

The versatility of a computer lies solely in the fact that it can be instructed to carry out many different tasks, each one through the program typed in. Designing (or writing) programs is both absorbing and challenging but alternatively they may be copied directly onto the keyboard from the growing number of articles in computer magazines. Equally books of programs are produced for the owner by "software houses" (a delightful name for people who sell computer programs), as a single example, specialist ones for teachers and parents for educating children, especially at primary level. This may not be quite such an easy way out as might be imagined for the odd mistake or printing error may give rise to a program which will not run. We will soon appreciate that every little detail is important, so much so that even a comma omitted or in the wrong place can upset the whole program. The need is therefore that even when copying a program some skill in entering it is desirable, there is nothing difficult in this, it just needs a little practice.

Going one step further taped programs can be purchased quite reasonably for the more complex jobs, they are designed by experts and are of such length that the alternative of typing them in ourselves would be frightening. The choice is ours but before getting down to the practicalities of programming let us first look at the ways and means so that we can better appreciate just how as ordinary domesticated mortals the computer has come within our grasp.

We might define a program simply as a set of instructions together with the appropriate data given to a computer.

5.2 Machine code programming

Consider first the simplest job of all, displaying a single character on the screen, for example, the letter Z. Machine (binary) code for Z is 01011010 (Section 3.2) and suppose that the binary instructions which switch the processor circuits for doing the job, i.e. holding the code in the memory, reading it continually and displaying it on the screen are 00100111. The instructions and data can therefore be contained in two bytes, 00100111 01011010. Given two keys only on the keyboard labelled 0 and 1 this machine-code can be entered and away we go.

The difficulty of keying in all these 0's and 1's correctly is obvious, moreover if this is the simplest instruction, what hope have we of entering a long program without mistakes? This is where the *hexadecimal* keyboard comes into play, the 16-key unit mentioned in Section 3.2. The new owner will not be using hexadecimal straightaway and probably never will so we need only know enough to avoid looking and feeling blank when the mysterious "HEX" is mentioned. Appendix 3 helps in the realization that HEX is only another numbering system following the same rules but with a radix of 16 (hex = 6 plus deci = 10). The happy outcome of the Appendix is that any 4-digit binary number can be represented by a single digit hexadecimal number so the two bytes reduce to 27 5A as seen from Appendix A5.1. The 16 keys are labelled 0----9, A----F, pressing any one causes the four corresponding binary digits (the machine code) to be transmitted.

5.3 High-level languages

Machine code is classed as a low-level language, every single move that the processor makes has to be communicated to it as a binary instruction. In fact there could be very many elementary operations in doing even the smallest calculation and to have to enter each of these in binary or hex would most certainly damp enthusiasm. There are several ways of simplifying the process but the one which is least demanding of the user is in fact a computer program *within* the computer, enabling programs to be written in a *high-level language* which it promptly changes to the low-level or machine language required by the processor. This most helpful internal computer program is known as an *interpreter* (i.e. it translates from one language into another) and as mentioned above, it is this device which simplifies computing for us all.

The interpreter program resides permanently within the ROM. With it the processor takes the English-like statements we enter and translates them into the appropriate binary codes which it understands and uses.

Accordingly the instructions are typed line by line and checked from the display or *listing* on the screen (or display panel in the case of a pocket computer). A back-up check is available from code signals also put on the screen by the computer showing that it considers all is well or conversely that it does not because the rules have been broken. In the latter case the corrections are made. The program goes into the memory (RAM) and eventually an order to execute it sets the processor working.

Within the processor the addresses of the instructions are stored in order in an electronic circuit known appropriately as an *Instruction Address Register* (also known as a *Program Counter*). This register sends out each memory address in turn via the address bus and the relative instructions find their way back via the data bus. The processor executes each instruction before causing its register to fetch the next. The results of the work are displayed on the screen in the manner directed by the programmer.

There are many high-level languages, each with a specific purpose, for example, for business or for science. One which has become surprisingly popular is known as BASIC, a title now unavoidable in the computer world. It is almost invariably used in personal computers and the letters stand for Beginners' All-Purpose Symbolic Instruction Code. BASIC was originally developed in the USA as a simple teaching language but its capabilities in producing highly complex programs with relative simplicity of use have endeared it to most microcomputer manufacturers. A little unfortunately perhaps there are variations, although generally minor. Nevertheless, for those about to take the plunge in what follows it is possible to learn some of the fundamentals of the language safe in the knowledge that whichever computer is purchased they will immediately feel at home with the instruction book.

One might now be tempted to ask why we should even consider programming in machine language when high-level languages have so much to offer. There are two main reasons. Firstly, the programs are executed many times faster which is of importance when they are long, and secondly less memory is used. It is therefore only the old hands at the game who need the HEX keyboard, none of us is in this category – yet!

Chapter Six

CHATTING IT UP

The topicality of the word "program" may lead one to expect a chapter full of simple BASIC programs, however our purpose is not to do this but to gain BASIC *insight* so that readers who do not possess a computer or who have only recently acquired one are put into the picture. The need arises because as indicated earlier, instruction books often leave us frustrated from getting bogged down by information written seemingly for the practitioner rather than the novice. For example, do we really understand "random", "modulus", "arctan" and "argument"? For the "haves" these remaining chapters may help to clarify some of the peculiar things which seem to arise in computer use, for the "have-nots" the notes are educational in that they provide an insight into the mysteries of programming and thus will help in deciding whether or not owning a computer is vital. True, one learns faster on a working system but remember that our aim is awareness rather than proficiency, that can come later. We will talk entirely in terms of a home computer with a normal video screen. For the pocket computer, techniques are a little different but it must be appreciated that the screen has simply given way to a display panel on which appears the current line only, the rest of the program being held in the memory but available line by line if required.

Thus we imagine a screen in front of us and a keyboard on which by dint of searching any of the characters or commands can be found. There are well over one hundred from which to select (up to 200 for computers which handle colour) so more than one key may need to be pressed for a single operation. In accordance with typewriter practice therefore many keys are labelled with upper and lower characters and probably with other functions, "shift" or other keys deciding which is to be selected. There should be no difficulty in following the instructions for operating the keyboard, much is self-evident. A RUBOUT or DELETE key allows us to hide our mistakes.

6.1 Bugs and Syntax

Before getting down to more practical moves we must appreciate that when an instruction is typed, the interpreter (Section 5.3) has to sort out exactly what is to be done, a single keyboard instruction usually resulting in many machine instructions. There is obviously a limit to the total number of different moves which can be made, hence programming languages restrict our freedom to a certain extent by keeping us to a set of rules. The alternative of allowing more freedom of expression by the user naturally leads to a longer program for the interpreter. Straying from the rules gets user and machine at cross-purposes but when inevitably mistakes are made computer jargon labels them as *bugs*, but a more refined description is *syntax errors*. "Syntax" may be defined for English composition as "a set of rules for the grammatical arrangement of words" and it applies to computer instructions in similar fashion for each component of an instruction must not only be there but also be in the right place. When errors creep in, the computer gives a reminder by displaying a *syntax error marker* (for example, a white-on-black S) at the point of error. Incidently if things get into too much of a muddle the computer can be switched off to clear everything and a fresh start made. Happily nothing done on the keyboard can actually damage a computer.

6.2 Cursors

This brings us to a very useful computer feature, the *cursor*. Its centuries-old meaning, "a running messenger" is most appropriate. In BASIC it may be, for example, a white-on-black letter at the appropriate position on the screen reminding the programmer as to what is required and where, e.g. K for keyword or command or L (letters) for the data to follow. These two alone help to ensure that the rules are followed and the cart never put before the horse. The cursor position also indicates where the next character typed will appear. A cursor most helpful in programming is the pointer ▶ which is an indicator of the line in a program which is of current interest. The cursors and syntax error marker in fact anticipate our wishes and keep us in order.

6.3 The answer back

Further help comes from *report codes* which appear at the bottom of the screen. They are an additional aid to the user by indicating why, for example, something did not go according to plan or why a program has stopped. The meanings of the symbols are set out in the instruction book.

6.4 Printing

To get in tune with the idea of typing in and how BASIC rules arise let us consider entering the headings of an expenditure account in the form

EXPENDITURE

DATE   ITEM   COST

On switching on, a K cursor appears in the bottom left-hand corner of the screen asking what the computer is required to *do*. There are many commands in BASIC either to be typed or on some machines given by depressing a single key. We wish to print letters on the screen so either type PRINT or press the PRINT key. PRINT now appears on the screen with a cursor change from say K to L. Now comes the first BASIC rule with regard to *strings*. A string is simply text or words (a string of characters) and the BASIC rule is that "strings must be enclosed within quotation marks" (just as this rule is). Accordingly the next move is to type a quotation mark (") followed by the word Expenditure (the string) and again a quotation mark. The stages so far are illustrated in Fig. 6.1(i) at 1 to 3. This completes the instruction and it can be viewed at the bottom of the screen to check, it has been entered but not yet carried out. On depression of, or touching the NEWLINE key (or other labels as shown in the Figure), the instruction is obeyed in this case simply to print the word EXPENDITURE at the top of the screen. The instruction disappears and a report code takes its place, with such a simple job to do the report code (which we can look up in the instruction book) is likely to indicate "no difficulty".

Suppose however that one of the quotation marks is omitted. The interpreter could not accept the instruction for clearly if a string is to be printed it must know both where it starts and finishes, therefore up pops the syntax error marker as shown in Fig. 6.1(ii) and the second quotation marks must be entered (the ▯ cursor is already in the right position) before acceptance is possible. By noting reports when they arise and observing the appropriate BASIC rules therefore, there should be no difficulty in making a start, getting in harmony with the machine comes with practice.

Notice from Fig. 6.1(i) that the title EXPENDITURE is printed at the left-hand end of the line, we in fact require it in the middle. This is accomplished by use of the TAB (tabulate) facility which is realised in the same way as with all other commands and functions, in this case by typing TAB or by pressing or touching a key so marked.

Each line on the screen comprises a certain number of characters depending on the particular computer as noted in Section 3.3, we will assume 32, labelled $\emptyset-31$. Imagine the line to be divided into 32 little boxes as shown in Fig. 6.1(iii) and by typing, say, TAB 1$\emptyset$ the string commences at the 11th box. The full instruction to be entered on the keyboard is also shown.

Now we can move down to the next line to be printed and again each computer has a certain number of lines, in this case we assume 22, although many computers have more. BASIC has a single command for placing characters anywhere on the screen, AT. Fig. 6.1(iv) now uses this to print all the headings

1. Switch on

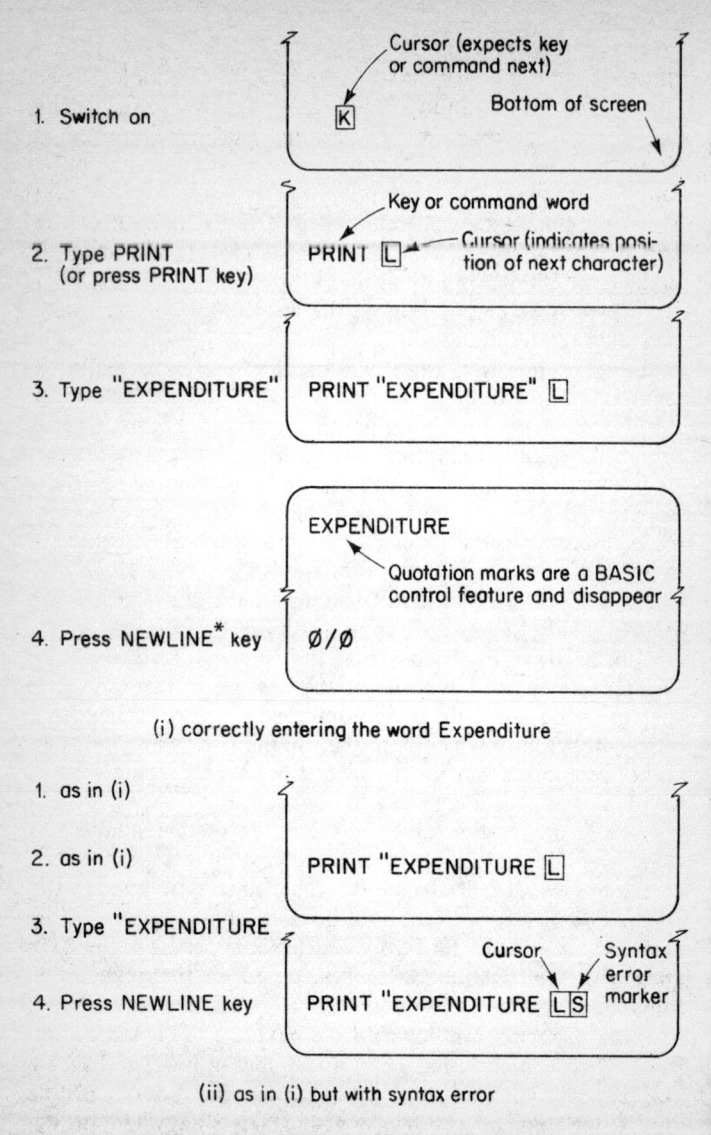

    K — Cursor (expects key or command next)
    Bottom of screen

2. Type PRINT
   (or press PRINT key)

    PRINT L
    Key or command word
    Cursor (indicates position of next character)

3. Type "EXPENDITURE"

    PRINT "EXPENDITURE" L

4. Press NEWLINE* key

    EXPENDITURE
    Quotation marks are a BASIC control feature and disappear
    Ø/Ø

(i) correctly entering the word Expenditure

1. as in (i)

2. as in (i)

    PRINT "EXPENDITURE L

3. Type "EXPENDITURE

4. Press NEWLINE key

    PRINT "EXPENDITURE L S
    Cursor   Syntax error marker

(ii) as in (i) but with syntax error

Fig. 6.1 Headings for expenditure account

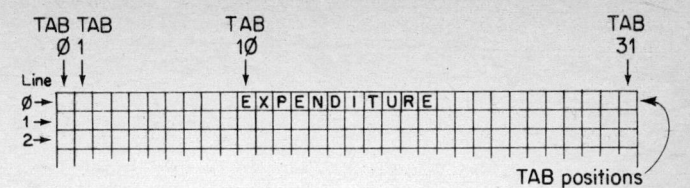

BASIC instruction → PRINT TAB 10; "EXPENDITURE"

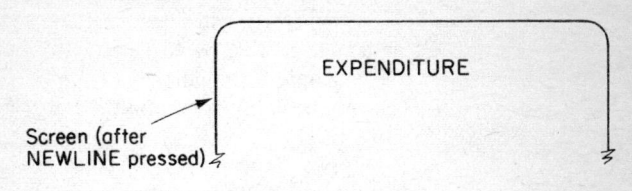

(iii) positioning title in line

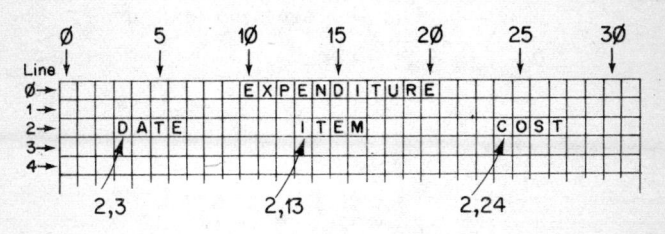

BASIC instruction → PRINT TAB 10; "EXPENDITURE"; AT 2,3; "DATE"; AT 2,13; "ITEM"; AT 2,24; "COST"

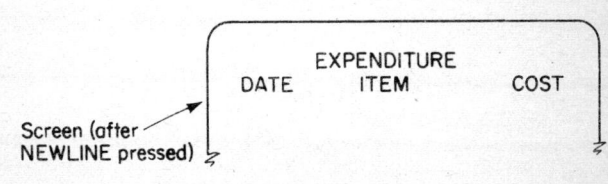

(iv) printing full heading

* other labels are ENTER, RETURN, ACCEPT

of the expenditure account. Screen positions must be quoted in the correct sequence, line/column so with lines 0−21 and columns 0−31 the top left-hand corner is ∅,∅, the top right-hand corner ∅,31 and the middle of the screen, say 11,15 (there is no exact middle with even numbers of lines and columns). The instruction is shown in the figure and note that it is littered with commas and semicolons. These need a little skill in handling for they cannot be used indiscriminately, examples in the instruction book will make this clear. Each may also be used as an instruction as to where to print the *next* character, for example, immediately following the previous one (;) or automatically to a certain TAB position as arranged by the manufacturer (,).

It all looks straightforward and it is. Mistakes made are soon rectified and fortunately we do learn from them.

So far, although in this introduction we have only looked at PRINT, TAB and AT, it is evident that talking to a computer is a two-way affair made foolproof by the signs (cursors, syntax error and report codes) fed back. Because of this reciprocal action between machine and programmer the modern computer is described as *interactive*.

Chapter Seven

THE BARE BONES OF BASIC – SINGLE INSTRUCTIONS

If a program is defined as a *set* of stored instructions, then a single instruction is not a program, hence this separate short chapter preceding the main one. BASIC allows us to use the home computer as a calculator although it must be admitted that if this is the only purpose, then a scientific calculator is more convenient.

7.1 Calculations

The first thing one notices is that although the keyboard shows the normal arithmetical *operators* + and –, it does not have x and ÷. The latter *operators* in computers are designated by * and /. Another change, obviously to avoid having to print the small index, is ** or ↑, meaning "raise to the power of". Examples are:

for	20 x 5	type in	20*5
	20 ÷ 5	" "	20/5
	20 + 5	" "	20 + 5 (no change)
	20 – 5	" "	20 – 5 (no change)
	20^5	" "	20**5
			(or 20 ↑ 5 on some computers)

Strange perhaps, but we soon get used to it, eventually almost as though x and ÷ were never invented.

Faced with the problem in school,

$$\text{calculate } \frac{369 \times 255}{14 \times 8.3}$$

we would have decided that nothing cancels so probably without much enthusiasm plodded through the calculation to discover the answer if we were lucky, of 809.77. With a computer such a calculation is simplicity itself, so we would type

   PRINT 369*255/14*8.3

but get the wrong answer for just as with calculators rules of entry must be followed. What the computer has made of the instruction is in fact

$$\frac{369 \times 255}{14} \times 8.3 .$$

What should be entered is

   PRINT 369*255/14/8.3

to get the immediate answer 809.76764. The instruction book is a reminder of the rules and if uncertain there is always resort to brackets for anything within them is calculated first and the result used subsequently, so with

   PRINT 369*255/(14*8.3) ,

14*8.3 is calculated first (116.2), the computer then continues with 369*255/116.2.

7.2 Accuracy

This is worth mentioning even though it may be of little interest to many users who are more concerned with programming than with long-winded calculations. The problem is, how can a computer which displays, for example, only an 8-digit number cope with a multiplication which results in more than 8 digits, such as 79533 x 8642? The answer is that it cannot with full accuracy for whereas the correct answer is 687,324,186, a typical home computer displays 687,324,190 and things get worse with higher numbers. However, to get things into perspective, if we look back a few years to before computers and calculators entered the home, even 7-figure logarithm tables would have resulted in less accuracy and most people had to be content with 4-figure tables for the 7-figure were a rarity.

Computers in fact handle very large numbers using scientific notation. This is fully covered in Appendix A1.1.

7.3 Trigonometry

With a computer, books of trigonometrical tables are no longer needed for it contains them all. Where some of us may be used for example, to $\sin^{-1} \theta$ representing "the angle whose sin is θ", computers almost invariably use arcsin θ (ASN), arcos θ (ACS) etc., again to avoid the inconvenience of the little -1. Angles are expressed in radians but we often need to work in degrees so, recalling that a radian is the angle subtended at the centre of a circle by an arc of length equal to the radius as shown in Fig. 7,1 then because there are 2π radii to the complete circumference, the circle of 360° also encloses 2π radians. Hence 1 radian is equivalent to

$$\frac{360}{2\pi} \quad \text{or} \quad \frac{180}{\pi}$$

(57.3) degrees. Thus if, for example, the value of tan 45° is required, then PRINT TAN (45*π/180) gets the answer 1.0 which of course we knew all the time. Note the brackets for otherwise the computer would calculate

$$\text{TAN 45 (radians)} \times \frac{\pi}{180},$$

a very different result.

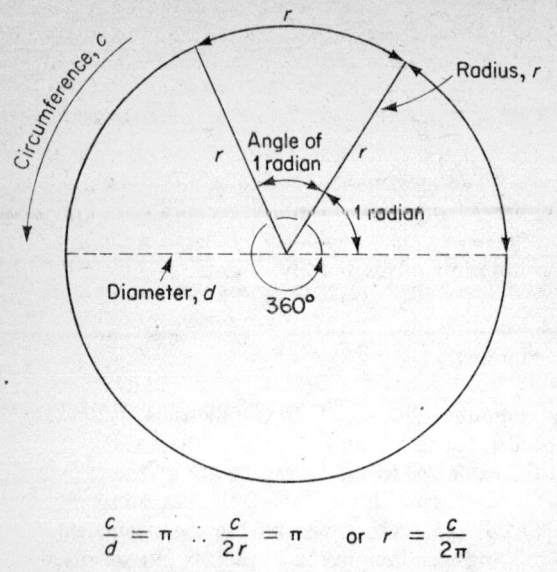

$$\frac{c}{d} = \pi \quad \therefore \quad \frac{c}{2r} = \pi \quad \text{or} \quad r = \frac{c}{2\pi}$$

i.e. there are 2π radii round a circle, hence 2π radians = $360°$

Fig. 7.1 Equivalence of radians and degrees

7.4 Random numbers

A BASIC feature used much more frequently than might be imagined is the generation of random numbers. A *random* number is one which within a certain range is as likely to occur as is any other number. The fascination of the roulette wheel springs from its random selection of a number from 1–36 (excluding the zero). The wheel is carefully designed for randomness, were it not so, there would be many experts around the gaming tables capable of detecting the bias and walking off with the profits. Asking the computer to print a random number (PRINT RND) results in one between 0 and 1 (typically to 8 decimal figures), this range can then be multiplied up, for example, by 100 then gives random numbers between 0 and 100.

7.5 Other functions

Apart from the various operators and functions already mentioned, several others are also available at the touch of a key, for example:

(i) SQR gives the square root.
(ii) INT (the *integer*) gets rid of all the figures to the right of the decimal point, for example PRINT INT 79.533 results in just 79. INT is quite a useful function and it gives us the opportunity of seeing what a computer can do. Suppose it has to replace a faulty roulette wheel, then the following stages demonstrate the use of the random and integer functions together. Note that the random number generated could possibly be 0 but never 1.

Instruction   *Result*

PRINT RND   random number between 0 and 1
  (*Example:* 0.26918030)

PRINT 36*RND   random number between 0 and 35.999999
  (*Example:* 9.6904908)

PRINT (36*RND) + 1   random number between 1 and 36.999999
  (*Example:* 10.690491)

PRINT INT(36*RND) + 1   random number between 1 and 36
  (*Example:* 10)

So the last instruction is equivalent to a spin of the roulette wheel and in the example quoted, number 10 comes up. (Note however that RND is not quite true random, for absolute perfection there is one more step.)

(iii) ABS (*absolute* value, also known as the modulus). *Modulus* and *argument* are better known to readers with a knowledge of vectors. We will not delve into this too deeply but generally the term "argument" can be taken as being synonymous with "operand" which means the quantity being operated on. ABS is the real or actual value of the argument which in fact simply involves removing the sign, thus both PRINT ABS 1.5 and PRINT ABS −1.5, result in the same, 1.5.

A reminder about epsilon (e) will not come amiss, it is the mysterious 2.71828 which occurs so frequently in Nature, hence in calculations in which *natural* phenomena are involved. BASIC provides natural (Napierian) logarithms (LN) which are to the base e and common logarithms (to be base 10) from these. e^x (EXP) is also available.

Lest one should now have the impression that the computer is only a device for rather complicated calculations, let us be reassured that this is not so, mathematical calculations are only a small part of its attributes. This facility is there for those who need but as has already been mentioned, it is the programmability which is the computer's greatest asset. This we consider next.

Chapter Eight

THE BARE BONES OF BASIC – PROGRAMS

From what has been said, it is evident that a program is no more than a list of single instructions telling the computer step by step what to do and in a language both we and the interpreter understand. The interpreter, through its own internal program rephrases the instructions into machine code for the processor. Evidently the instructions must be in some sort of order so each separate one is given a number and the computer obeys in numerical order. The advice always given to the programmer is to leave spaces in the numbering scheme so that further instructions may be interposed later on if required. A generally accepted arrangement is therefore to label the instructions 10, 20, 30 . . . rather than 1, 2, 3 . . . .

As each instruction is typed in it appears at the bottom of the screen where it can be checked. Subsequently on pressing NEWLINE (or whatever "go ahead" code is used) it reappears at the top of the screen with the rest of the program and in numerical order which the computer checks and arranges. The instructions are stored in the memory to await the signal RUN (followed by NEWLINE etc.) whereupon they are carried out and the result displayed on the screen. This is only one of the many ways computer output is used, it could also be fed to a printer for a printed copy or used for control in so many ways, for example, in the home for operating a model railway, on the streets with traffic lights or in the factory for operating robots.

Accordingly, as each instruction is added, the program grows at the top of the screen until the latter is full whereupon the whole program automatically moves up with the earlier items disappearing out of the top as new ones are added at the bottom. Nothing is lost, even though not displayed, the first instructions are still held in the memory. If changes need to be made to the program an EDIT facility enables the programmer to bring down any particular line to the bottom and make changes. NEWLINE (etc.) then puts that line back into its right place.

Before looking at the various facilities at the programmer's disposal we might consider one BASIC instruction which the computer does not obey but simply stores and prints only when listing the program. It is the REM (remark) statement which is used by the programmer simply to title or clarify parts of the program. Hence

```
10   REM        PRICE LIST
20   PRINT      "PLEASE ENTER ITEM"
```

shows how a program may begin and when run, line 10 is ignored so effectively starting at line 20.

8.1 Variables

Many programs are written to take different sets of data but carry out the same work, a very simple example is the determination of petrol consumption of a vehicle in litres per kilometre (or miles per gallon). For this, two quantities must be entered, the number of litres (or gallons) and the number of kilometres (or miles). These values are different on each run, they are known as (numerical) *variables*. BASIC can handle many of these in a program. When a variable is entered it is given a label which the programmer can choose with due regard to the labelling rules, for example, with numerical variables, a single letter or word.

Variables are entered via two different instructions, LET and INPUT. As an example, the instruction LET R = 5 causes the processor to *label* a section of memory as R and *enter* into that memory the number 5. We see this in action in a very simple program:

```
10   LET R = 8
20   LET C = π*2*R
30   PRINT "THE CIRCUMFERENCE OF A CIRCLE
     OF RADIUS   "; R;" IS ";C
```

In line 10 the computer is asked to assign a block of memory to a variable and label it R so that it can be recalled at any time by simply quoting R. In that memory the number 8 is to be stored. Line 20 recalls the value in R, multiplies it by 2π and asks for the result to be stored in a separate block of memory to be labelled C. Line 30 shows that strings (between the inverted commas) and variables (no inverted commas) can be printed in succession. On entering the instruction RUN, the screen display changes to:

THE CIRCUMFERENCE OF A CIRCLE OF RADIUS 8
IS 5Ø.265483

[Note that in the program there is a space after RADIUS and one on each side of IS to avoid the result . . . RADIUSIS5Ø.265483.]

If the circumference for any other radius is required, pressing NEWLINE again brings the program back onto the screen, the first line can then be edited to change the 8 to the new value. Hardly good computer practice, there must be a better way. There is by use of the INPUT statement:

```
10   INPUT R
20   LET C = π*2*R
30   . . . as in previous program
```

INPUT R says that the user will provide the data for the variable R, accordingly at line 10 the computer stops and waits for the user to type the value of R and when this is entered the program is completed. Now it is possible to use the program over and over again by simply "inputting" each different value for the radius. Variables are an extremely useful feature in programming and few programs will be seen without LET and/or INPUT statements. Lest the reader should come across the statement so often used for example,

LET R = R + 1

and begins to feel at odds with previous understanding of

mathematics, it actually means "add 1 to the previous value of R and now let this be the new value of R". We will see this happening in the next section.

Textual variables (or *literal*, i.e. composed of letters) follow the same principles. Strings can be assigned to variables provided that the label chosen has the form of a single letter followed by the single stroke dollar sign, for example, B$, W$ (with some computers the other way round, i.e. $B, $W). A single example serves to show the use:

```
10  LET A$ = "***"
20  LET B$ = "HISTORY"
30  PRINT A$; B$; A$
```

to obtain the display

```
***HISTORY***
```

where *** is made into a string, assigned to the variable A$ and used twice in line 30. There is little gain in so doing in this particular example but usually a variable is used many times as will be seen in later programs.

8.2 Loops

Program loops have their equivalence in many facets of everyday life. Those who get caught for the job of washing up know this only too well. Their program might be considered to run as follows:

1. Run hot water into bowl.
2. Run cold water into bowl.
3. Add washing-up liquid.
4. Take item of crockery or cutlery.
5. Wash.
6. Rinse.
7. Place in drainer.
8. Flush away dirty water.
9. Clean bowl.

But this only washes one item so clearly after line 7 the washer-up returns to 4 and repeats the 4—7 path until all items have been cleaned whereupon the program is completed by 8 and 9. The repetitive phase is said to be effected by *looping*. BASIC has a simple way of diverting the processor to an instruction not in sequence, it is GOTO and in the program above would appear after 7, simply saying GOTO 4.

So far so good, but surely the processor will keep going round the loop and never get out. This is so as the following would demonstrate:

```
10   LET N = 1
20   PRINT N;" ";
30   LET N = N + 1
40   GOTO 20
```

Here line 10 assigns 1 to the variable labelled N. Line 20 therefore prints the figure 1 followed by a space. Line 30 increases the quantity in N by 1 so that now N = 2. Line 40 returns to line 20, hence 2 is printed followed by a space and it is evident that the whole screen fills with consecutive numbers starting from 1 until the computer cries halt because there is no space left.

Looping and breaking out are accomplished by two main methods, the *conditional* which we look at in the next section and the FOR, NEXT instruction. With the latter two things are quoted, a variable label and its range, for example, FOR C = 1 TO 20 in which C is the variable label and 1—20 the range. In this case the FOR instruction causes the computer to set up a counter under the label C and running from 1 to 20. The loop is repeated on meeting the later instruction NEXT C until 20 cycles through the loop have been executed. The looping then ceases so in

```
10   LET N = 1
20   FOR C = 1 TO 20
30   PRINT N;" ";
40   LET N = N + 1
50   NEXT C
```

lines 20 and 50 arrest the looping when all numbers up to and including 20 have been printed on the screen. But what if letters are to be printed instead of numbers? This is allowed for in most machines by quoting in the instruction book the code number for each character, in a typical case letter A is shown to have a code number 38; B, 39 up to Z, 63. By the simple expedient of PRINT CHR$ 38, letter A is printed, PRINT CHR$ 40 for letter C and so on. CHR$ is the special function for this particular purpose. Hence

```
10   LET N = 38
20   FOR C = 1 TO 26
30   PRINT CHR$ N;" ";
40   LET N = N + 1
50   NEXT C
```

on this particular computer will print the letters of the alphabet.

8.3 Conditionals

As already mentioned looping also ceases when a conditional statement becomes effective. The conditional is immediately recognized by the IF statement, one of major importance because it allows the computer to make a decision based on the conditions in the program and the input data. Firstly let us use the conditional to break out of the above program by letting it replace the FOR,NEXT instruction:

```
10   LET N = 38
20   PRINT CHR$ N;" ";
30   LET N = N + 1
40   IF N<64 THEN GOTO 20
```

and again, on a computer using this particular coding for its alphabetical characters (38 for A to 63 for Z), the full alphabet is printed. In line 40 < stands for "is less than", it is the standard mathematical symbol as is > for "greater than".

Presuming that by now we are getting used to the *general* idea of programming, we next see the conditional IF in a different program and sort it out afterwards. This small program embodies several features already discussed and introduces just two more of the many facilities BASIC offers:

```
10   FOR C = 1 TO 20
20   LET R = RND
30   IF R >= .5 THEN PRINT "HEAD"
40   IF R < .5 THEN PRINT "TAIL"
50   PAUSE 100
60   CLS
70   PAUSE 50
80   NEXT C
```

C is chosen as the label for the counting variable (1 to 20) for the FOR,NEXT statement introduced in line 10 and operative at line 80. Line 20 assigns the value of the random number (between 0 and 1) generated by RND to a variable labelled R. The random number is as likely to be below 0.5 as it is to be equal to or above and lines 30 and 40 ask the computer to make the decision whether to print Head or Tail. Line 50 uses a statement new to us, PAUSE, which stops computing for a time according to the number following. This is in terms of the number of frames of the display per second. Don't be too concerned about this, it is usually the same as the power mains *frequency*, 50 cycles per second generally but 60 in USA, Canada and some other countries. In this case the display of HEAD or TAIL remains on the screen for 100/50, i.e. 2 seconds. In line 60 CLS (clear screen) does just that for one second as instructed by line 70. Line 80 returns the processing to the beginning of the loop at line 20. This happens 20 times as regulated by line 10 whereupon the display ceases. Thus the program "tosses a coin" 20 times and announces each result. Removal of line 60 allows all 20 results to remain printed on the screen in a column.

8.4 PEEK and POKE

It is hardly right not to mention these two instructions because both titles seem to receive much publicity, perhaps because they have a hint of the dramatic. But they aptly describe the work done which is to peer or PEEK into the memory, or alternatively to push or POKE data into it. They are simply two additional facilities but perhaps not used seriously until some programming expertise has been gained, nevertheless they are very handy, especially for saving memory.

The instruction book probably contains information on which memory addresses are in use and for what, so to see what is stored in any particular location the programmer need only enter, for example,

```
PRINT PEEK 8017
```

Let us imagine that we are using a computer in which memory address 8017 contains the second row down of letter E in the character generator portion of the ROM as shown in Fig. 4.2(i). In this case, the result of the instruction will be the decimal number 126 and if we work out the binary code for this we should come up with ∅1111110 (Section 2.2), just as shown in the figure. Needless to say, a simple program can be written, not only to print out the numbers corresponding to what is stored in several memory addresses in succession but also to convert each number to binary, this is how the display as shown in the figure is obtained (see also Section 4.1).

POKE on the other hand allows the programmer to enter data directly into a memory location which is quoted in the same way as for PEEK — but nothing can be entered into the ROM of course. The number representing the data to be inserted must not exceed 255 otherwise more than 8 binary digits are involved.

8.5 Graphics

Graphics is a general title for the pictorial side of computers through which drawings, graphs and games are produced, both moving and stationary and with some machines, also in colour. The facilities available vary widely with different computers, but for most the main principles are the same, what differs is the degree of sophistication. But we keep things simple here.

The smallest element or dot which can be displayed is known as a *pixel* (picture element) and clearly the smaller the pixel, the better the *resolution* or "faithfulness" of the display. This is illustrated by Fig. 8.1 where the smaller pixel is seen to describe the same curve more precisely although many more pixels are needed. Any display on the screen must also be held in the memory for this is where it comes from. More pixels imply more memory, therefore the price to be paid for higher resolution is in the additional memory absorbed. The more expensive computers give the user a choice in pixel size so that the best compromise between resolution and memory required can be made.

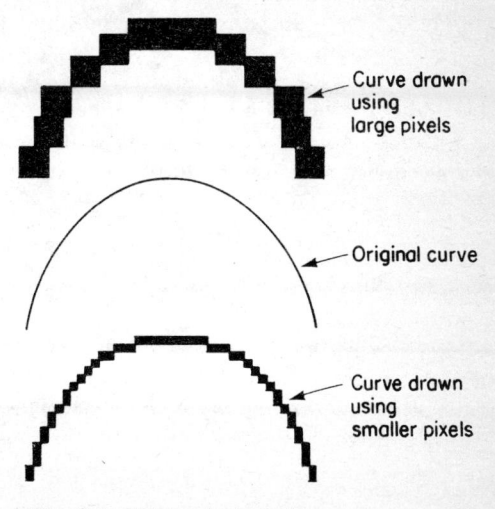

Fig. 8.1 Effect of pixel size

We saw in Fig. 6.1(iv) how the screen is divided horizontally and vertically into lines and columns for positioning alphanumeric characters (letters and numbers). The same technique holds for pixels but now because the pixel is smaller than a character the numbers get bigger and in fact range for home computers from some 48 x 40 to as many as 640 x 256 (columns/lines). As an example of the smaller pixel sizes, recalling from Fig. 4.2(iii) that a character may be generated with an area subdivided into 8 x 8 dots, then if each dot is used as a pixel as it is in some personal computers, then a 32 x 22 (columns/lines) screen accommodates (32 x8)x (22 x 8), i.e. 256 x 176 pixels. In addition many computers have a selection of pixel shapes. Taking one of the simplest however, such as the screen shown in Fig. 6.1(iv) which has 32 columns x 22 lines, with a square pixel of one quarter the area of a character, then the screen pixel numbering runs Ø–63 for the columns and Ø–43 for the lines. For plotting points however we should not refer to columns and lines but to x and y co-ordinates and in accordance with what we learned at school about graphs and where to draw the axes (some revision is in Appendix 4), the x co-ordinate is measured from the left and the y upwards from the bottom. Fig. 8.2 shows how the position of any of the 64 x 44 = 2816 pixels is described and the simple instruction to the computer, PLOT 5Ø,3Ø results in a tiny black square in the corresponding position on the screen. A horizontal straight line one pixel thick at y = 1Ø is drawn from:

```
1Ø   FOR X = Ø TO 63
2Ø   PLOT X,1Ø
3Ø   NEXT X
```

as shown in the figure. Here on the first run through the loop one pixel is plotted at Ø,1Ø (line 2Ø), on the second run at 1,1Ø, then at 2,1Ø up to 63,1Ø, the computer apparently drawing a horizontal straight line. Vertical lines are drawn similarly. Evidently, if in line 2Ø a function of y is used, then the graph of y is drawn. We can here examine the very simple graph of $y = \sqrt{x}$. With, for example, the scales used in Fig.

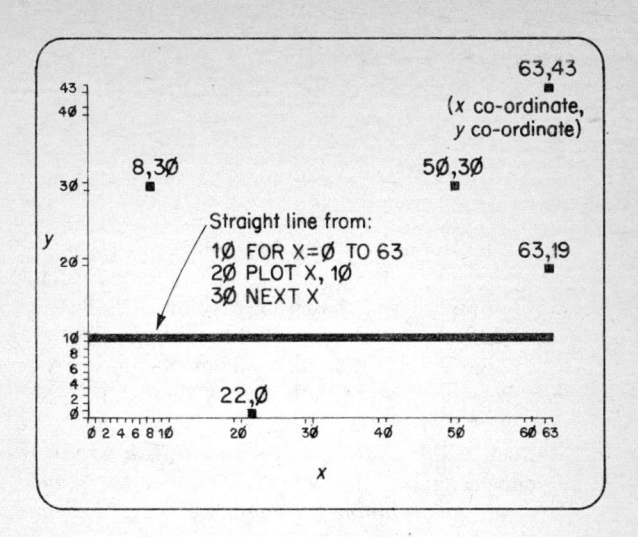

Fig. 8.2 Positioning pixels on a screen

8.2, because when x reaches 63, y is still less than 8, we should find that the y scale is not being used efficiently. When a graph is drawn on paper the scales are chosen to suit so that it fills the paper and neither huddles at the bottom nor shoots straight out of the top. With a computer however, the scales are fixed but what can be done is to multiply or divide the values of y. Thus in the following example, because with the particular scales being used the graph of $\sqrt{x}$ would be squashed along the bottom, it is multiplied by 5 and so fills the screen suitably. This is in fact equivalent to changing the scale for y:

```
10   FOR N = 0 TO 63
20   PLOT N, 5*SQR N
30   NEXT N
```

From these small beginnings one can appreciate how bigger programs are created with lines being drawn, spots moving and objects shifting about so given a modicum of programming experience, challenging computer games can be set up.

8.6 Summary

We could in fact go on for ever but that is not the purpose of the book. Enough of the simple beginnings of programming has been developed for the term no longer to be one shrouded in mystery. Indeed, what has been developed surely shows that given a little understanding of the underlying computer processes, programming presents no complications. As we have seen, programs can accomplish many things but for some home computer owners the delight may be less in the final outcome than in the struggle to get it. Suffice to say that we have only scratched the surface of programming and to keep things within the bounds of simplicity, quite deliberately no explanation has been included of some other essential facilities such as *subroutines* (small programs within the main one which can be picked up as often as is required), *arrays* (sets of variables, all under one name but each distinguished by its own subscript) and others. Altogether BASIC instructions make the computer a very versatile instrument indeed.

Chapter Nine

STORING PROGRAMS

In Section 4.5 a promise is made for a further look into the technique of tape storage of programs. It is a facility of no small value for imagine the frustration of having worked for perhaps an hour or two on a program, only to lose it all when the computer has to be switched off. The agony increases when a domestic television set is part of the outfit for an early switch-off may be imperative to avoid an uproar when the favourite tv programme is at risk.

The advantages of working in binary are touched on in Chapter Two, the feasibility of shifting a program out of a computer onto a magnetic recording tape provides another example for with binary signals it is a relatively uncomplicated and error-free process. A cassette tape records *audio* signals, usually speech or music but in this case the electronic equivalent of tones (or whistles) in short bursts to represent the binary $\emptyset$'s and 1's. We might imagine this to be the equivalent of the computer playing extremely short bursts of two piano notes a couple of octaves apart, one representing $\emptyset$ and the other 1. The rate of transfer between computer and cassette recorder varies with the particular model but think perhaps in terms of between 100 and 200 bits per second, so because 8 bits are contained within each memory location, the contents of some 12–24 locations (on average about 1–2 program lines) are sent out each second. Once the program is on the tape it is safe provided that we do nothing silly, such as recording another item over it. This is easily done if the tapes are not labelled sensibly. The program on the cassette can be played back into the computer time and time again. Using the simple analogy of the two paino notes, the computer is now listening to them and by writing $\emptyset$'s and 1's accordingly, sets up the original machine code program.

Looking now at the practical side and considering a computer which is designed for use with a domestic cassette recorder (i.e. does not have one built in), then connecting leads with plugs are needed and we can expect these to be supplied by the manufacturer. Fig. 9.1 shows at the top the elements of a recording system. The cassette is essentially a length of magnetizable plastic tape which can be wound and rewound between two reels, examination of one soon shows how it works. By "magnetizable" is meant that it can pick up magnetism just as does a steel pin when stroked by a magnet. A *record head* fed with electronic signals from a microphone or radio receiver impresses the magnetization along the tape and subsequently a *replay head* "reads" this and amplifiers reproduce the tiny signals picked up in much greater form for driving the loudspeaker (a single record/replay head may also be used). The magnetism can be removed by an *erase head* which automatically operates just before a recording is made (not shown in the figure).

Even though a built-in microphone may be provided there

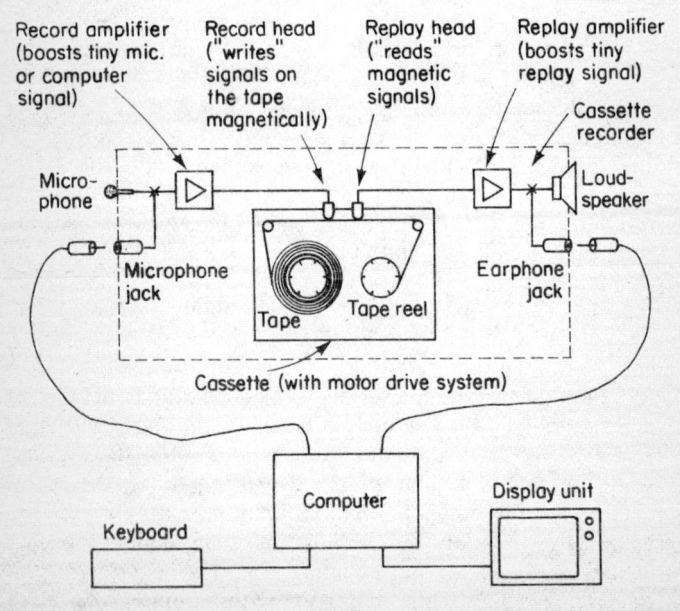

Fig. 9.1 Storing programs on magnetic tape

is usually a microphone *jack* fitted (the hole into which we push a plug) and this is the input which the computer is likely to use. Similarly, although a loudspeaker is included there is usually a jack which cuts it off when a plug connected to earphones is inserted. It is via this jack that the recorder plays back a program into the computer. Thus leads are connected between the computer and recorder as shown in the figure.

In BASIC the program will probably need a label or name and the REM statement is useful when several programs are held on one tape. With the system connected up as in the figure and the program displayed, all that is required is to switch on the cassette recorder set to "Record" and then use the command SAVE followed by the program title, for example, SAVE "ROULETTE". The program is then duplicated onto the tape in machine code usually within seconds to a minute or so, completion of the process being indicated by a report on the screen. In the reverse direction the command is LOAD followed by the title and with the tape rewound and the recorder switched to "Play", the program is fed back in. This is also all that is required when a program is purchased already on tape. That the program is actually on the tape can be checked by playing it back through the normal loudspeaker. The sequence of bits can then be heard as a raucous and squeaky musical buzz.

A little experience and juggling with cassette recorder volume controls may be needed but given clear advice from the instruction book, all should be well and the enjoyment of building up a personal library of programs begins.

IN CONCLUSION

It surely must be that having read this book, readers with no experience of computers whatsoever will feel better at ease when they meet one. The computer has been many years in its development and today it is a highly sophisticated instrument, probing its depths fully comes only with experience, patience and tenacity. We are not all summoned to be computer intellectuals so if the book has helped the reader to decide that he or she has *not* received the call, well and good. At least that reader will no longer feel like an outcast when the subject comes up. But if on the other hand the call has come and there is inspiration to go further then so much the better. "Tall oaks from little acorns grow."

Appendix 1

EXPONENTS

Even though our arithmetic may have suffered the ravages of time, we surely cannot have forgotten that two squared equals four and ten squared equals one hundred, written numerically as $2^2 = 4$, $10^2 = 100$. Another way of expressing this is

> 2 to the power of 2 = 4

and 10 to the power of 2 = 100.

Similarly,

> 2 to the power of 3 = 8

and 10 to the power of 3 = 1000.

The *exponent* (also known as the *index*) is the little raised number stating what power of a factor is to be taken, for example, in $2^3 = 8$, 3 is the exponent showing that three twos are multiplied together, i.e. $2^3 = 2 \times 2 \times 2$.

When the exponent is 2 we say that the number is *squared*; when the exponent is 3 we say that the number is *cubed*; when the exponent is 4, 5, 6 ..., we say that the number is *raised to the 4th, 5th, 6th ... power*.

Working in the opposite direction, if, for example, $2^3 = 8$, then the cube root of 8 is 2, written as $\sqrt[3]{8} = 2$ or using an exponent instead, $8^{\frac{1}{3}} = 2$.

Now $2^3 \times 2^2 = 2^5$ (5 twos multiplied together), a simple reminder that in multiplication the exponents are *added*.

Also

$$2^3 \div 2^2 = 2^1 \left(\frac{2 \times 2 \times 2}{2 \times 2} = 2 \right),$$

for division the exponents are subtracted. From this, since

$$\frac{2^3}{2^2} = 2^{(3-2)} = 2^{3+(-2)} = 2^3 \times 2^{-2}$$

(exponents added implies multiplication), then

$$\frac{1}{2^2} \text{ can be written as } 2^{-2},$$

equally

$$\frac{1}{2^{-2}} = 2^2$$

Finally,

$$2^4 = 16$$
$$2^3 = 8$$
$$2^2 = 4$$
$$2^1 = 2 \text{ (any number to the power of 1 is unchanged).}$$
$$2^0 = 1 \text{ (any number to the power of 0 equals 1)}$$

$$2^{-1} = \frac{1}{2^1} = 0.5$$

$$2^{-2} = \frac{1}{2^2} = 0.25$$

$$2^{-3} = \frac{1}{2^3} = 0.125$$

showing that each reduction of the exponent by 1 divides the result by 2. A table of powers of 2 follows in Appendix A5.2.

A1.1 Scientific notation

Because they are limited in the number of digits which can be displayed as a single number, scientific calculators and computers adopt *scientific notation*. Take the number 12345 as an example, the expressions below all have exactly the same value:

12345
12345 × 1 (i.e. × 10^0)
1234.5 × 10 (i.e. × 10^1)
123.45 × 100 (i.e. × 10^2)
12.345 × 1000 (i.e. × 10^3) and so on.

Also

123450 × 0.1 (i.e. × 10^{-1})
1234500 × 0.01 (i.e. × 10^{-2})

Scientific notation simply writes the power of 10 in each case in normal figures to avoid the difficulty of displaying it as a small raised number. Most computers automatically move to scientific notation when a number exceeds their display capacity and use a capital E to show when this occurs, e.g. 12.345 E + 3 really means 12.345 × 10^3, the E in fact standing for "times 10 to the power of". Negative exponents are treated similarly, e.g. 12.345 E −2 stands for 12.345 × 10^{-2}, i.e. 0.12345. Scientific calculators which can only display numbers omit the E and the two examples above simply read 12.345 03 and 12.345 −02. The number may also be automatically *normalized* by displaying it with a single digit to the left of the decimal point, e.g. 12.345 E3 entered would be displayed as 1.2345 E4, while 12.345 E−2 becomes 1.2345 E−1. The notation therefore enables very large or very small numbers to be manipulated.

Appendix 2

MORE ABOUT BINARY

Section 2.2 introduces us to binary notation showing that it follows the same rules as those which we use daily for decimals. One therefore might reasonably expect to find the same methods in use for addition, subtraction, multiplication and division and to give confidence that this is so we go one stage further. Following this in Appendix 5 are tables of binary equivalents.

A2.1 Binary addition

Firstly a reminder of the steps taken in adding decimal numbers, say, 3829, 2952 and 8713. To see what happens let us put them into a table with columns labelled according to the value represented by unity (1), for example, the 9 in the first number has a true value of 9×10^0, i.e. 9, whereas the 3 has a value of 3×10^3, i.e. 3000.

10^4	10^3	10^2	10^1	10^0	
	3	8	2	9	
	2	9	5	2	} Numbers being added
	8	7	1	3	
	2		1		Carry
1	5	4	9	4	Result

Adding the 10^0 column, $9 + 2 + 3 = 14$. This in fact is $(1 \times 10^1) + (4 \times 10^0)$ so 4 remains in the 10^0 column with 1 proper to the 10^1 column and *carried over* into it. Again for this column, $2 + 5 + 1 + 1 = 9$, no carry. For the 10^2

column, 8 + 9 + 7 = 24, 4 remains with 2 carried over. Next a total of 15 for the 10^3 column leaving 5 with a 1 carried over into a 10^4 column which for this particular calculation must be provided.

Addition of binary numbers is no different. Let us add the three numbers shown in the table below:

	Numbers being added	Carry	Result
2^0 (1)	0 0 1		1
2^1 (2)	1 0 0		1
2^2 (4)	1 1 1		1
2^3 (8)	1 0 0	1	0
2^4 (16)	1 1 1	1	0
2^5 (32)	0 1 0	1+1	1
2^6 (64)	1 0 1	1	1
2^7 (128)	0 0 0	1	1
Decimal equivalents →	94 52 85		231

69

We need not analyse this except to note that a 1 is carried for every 2 in the sum (note especially the carry from the 2^4 column).

This single comparison serves to make the point that binary arithmetic is based on the same rules as for decimal. There are some artful dodges built into computers to simplify matters but the fundamentals are unchanged. Perhaps obvious but worth noting is that in multiplication, $\emptyset \times \emptyset = \emptyset$, $\emptyset \times 1 = \emptyset$, $1 \times 1 = 1$.

A2.2 Binary permutations

Frequently in computer work, especially in memory addressing (Section 4.3) it is necessary to know the number of *different* arrangements of which a set of n binary digits is capable. For example, if n = 4, we wish to know how many 4-figure binary codes can be created with each different from all others. This problem is best approached by considering that when n = 1 there are, of course, 2 arrangements, $\emptyset$ and 1. For n = 2, then if the first digit is $\emptyset$ it can be followed by either $\emptyset$ or 1, also if the first digit is 1 it too can be followed by either $\emptyset$ or 1. Hence for n = 2, there are twice as many different combinations than for n = 1. This process can be continued as far as is desired but here we are looking for the mathematical relationship so let us summarize this so far and go one stage further only as developed in Fig. A2.1.

We need not go beyond n = 3 for it is obvious that each new step multiplies the number of different arrangements of the preceding step by 2 and because n is the number of digits in the number the last column in the figure indicates that there are 2^n arrangements possible.

A table of values of 2^n is given in Appendix A5.2.

Composition of binary number	Notes	Different arrangements possible	Number of arrangements
1 digit only (n = 1)	Two choices only →	Ø 1	2
2 digits (n = 2)	Equivalent to 1 digit with its 2 choices followed by 1 digit also with 2 choices →	ØØ Ø1 1Ø 11	2 x 2 (= 2^2)
3 digits (n = 3)	Equivalent to 2 digits with their 4 choices followed by 1 digit with 2 choices →	ØØØ ØØ1 Ø1Ø Ø11 1ØØ 1Ø1 11Ø 111	4 x 2 (= 2^3)

Fig. A.2.1 Binary permutations

Appendix 3

HEXADECIMAL

Because one of our aims is not to look ignorant when commonly used computer terms arise, we look at hexadecimal notation but only briefly. It is a useful exercise because it provides a constant reminder that without special arrangements (as discussed in Section 5.3) we have to talk to the processor in its own (machine) language. Our appreciation of binary leads directly to hexadecimal, the rules are identical, only the radix is changed.

For a radix of 16, that number of symbols is required and those chosen consist of the ten decimal numbers 0–9 plus the first six letters of the alphabet A–F. The sequence can be seen from the table in Appendix 5.1. A single example is all we need, say, 72DF in "hex" is equivalent to:

16^3 (4096)	16^2 (256)	16^1 (16)	16^0 (1)
7	2	D	F

← decimal equivalents

i.e. $(7 \times 4096) + (2 \times 256) + (13 \times 16) + (15 \times 1)$.
= 28672 + 512 + 208 + 15 = 29,407.
(D_{16} has the decimal equivalent of 13, F_{16} has the decimal equivalent of 15 – see Appendix A5.1.)

Because 4-digit binary numbers cover the 16 decimal numbers 0–15, one 4-digit binary number can be expressed by a single hex number so to convert $72DF_{16}$ to binary we simply substitute the appropriate 4-digit binary code for each hex digit, i.e.

hex →   7   2   D   F

binary → Ø111 ØØ1Ø 11Ø1 1111

$= 29,407_{10}$

and vice versa. The table in Appendix 5.1 may be of help.

Appendix 4

GRAPH CO-ORDINATES

Herein is revision on how a graph is drawn, mainly so that we fully appreciate the term *co-ordinate*. Co-ordinates are simply the magnitudes used to fix the position of a point, in this case, in a plane. Thus, given a square sheet of paper ABCD as in Fig. A4.1(i), the position of the point P can be determined in two ways.

(i) the perpendicular of P from AB (or CD) together with that from AD (or BC);
(ii) the distance from any corner, for example at A, and the angle the line joining P to A makes with either AB or AD.

Given the magnitudes obtained in (i) or (ii), P can subsequently be positioned.

The computer screen can be likened to a sheet of paper, but because for several reasons we cannot work from the edges, two *axes* are drawn or imagined, usually along the bottom and at the left-hand side as shown in (ii) of the figure. They are labelled x (axis) and y (axis) and are at right angles to each other. Any point P is stated by its x and y co-ordinates as shown. These are also known as the *cartesian* co-ordinates (after René Descartes, the French philosopher). This is the system used as an example in the main text (Section 8.5) but in programming the polar co-ordinates are also frequently used. These are shown in the figure as OP and the $\angle \theta$.

Therefore to plot a graph, which is simply a line demonstrating how one quantity varies relative to another, the computer takes each value of x and calculates the corresponding value of y, then through the PLOT instruction places a point on the screen.

As a reminder, examples of the simplest of graphs are shown in Fig. A4.1(iii):

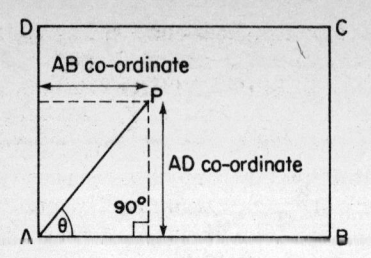

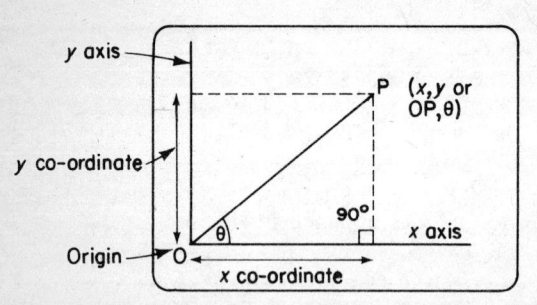

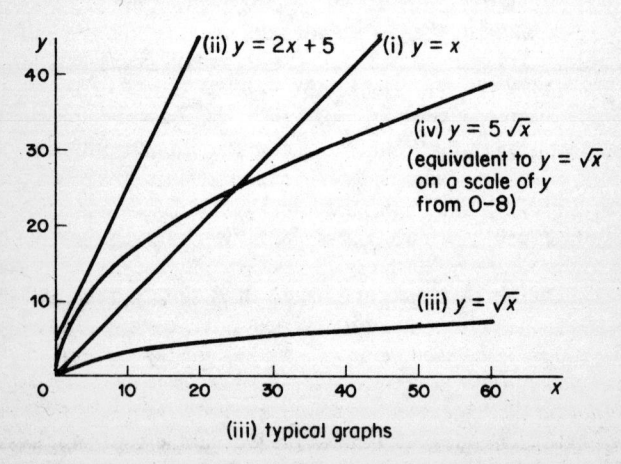

Fig. A.4.1 Plotting graphs

(i) $y = x$ is a straight line commencing at the origin, O;
(ii) $y = 2x + 5$ is of the general form $y = mx + c$, has a finite value when $x = 0$. It also demonstrates that a change of scale for y might be advantageous;
(iii) $y = \sqrt{x}$ shows again the effect of fixed scales and at
(iv) $y = 5\sqrt{x}$ shows the improvement when the graph is multiplied by 5, this being equivalent to dividing the y scale by the same amount. A program for plotting this is contained in Section 8.5.

Appendix 5

TABLES

It is not expected that we as novices will need to use these particular tables to any great extent but it is a fact that a glance over them helps to impress on us the order of things. The tables are also useful for checking answers when things are worked out for ourselves.

A5.1 Table of Decimal, Binary and Hexadecimal Equivalents

Decimal	Binary	Hexa-decimal	Decimal	Binary	Hexa-decimal
0	0	0	21	10101	15
1	1	1	22	10110	16
2	10	2	23	10111	17
3	11	3	24	11000	18
4	100	4	25	11001	19
5	101	5	26	11010	1A
6	110	6	27	11011	1B
7	111	7	28	11100	1C
8	1000	8	29	11101	1D
9	1001	9	30	11110	1E
10	1010	A	31	11111	1F
11	1011	B	32	100000	20
12	1100	C	33	100001	21
13	1101	D	34	100010	22
14	1110	E	35	100011	23
15	1111	F	36	100100	24
16	10000	10	37	100101	25
17	10001	11	38	100110	26
18	10010	12	39	100111	27
19	10011	13	40	101000	28
20	10100	14	41	101001	29

Decimal	Binary	Hexa-decimal	Decimal	Binary	Hexa-decimal
42	101010	2A	76	1001100	4C
43	101011	2B	77	1001101	4D
44	101100	2C	78	1001110	4E
45	101101	2D	79	1001111	4F
46	101110	2E	80	1010000	50
47	101111	2F	81	1010001	51
48	110000	30	82	1010010	52
49	110001	31	83	1010011	53
50	110010	32	84	1010100	54
51	110011	33	85	1010101	55
52	110100	34	86	1010110	56
53	110101	35	87	1010111	57
54	110110	36	88	1011000	58
55	110111	37	89	1011001	59
56	111000	38	90	1011010	5A
57	111001	39	91	1011011	5B
58	111010	3A	92	1011100	5C
59	111011	3B	93	1011101	5D
60	111100	3C	94	1011110	5E
61	111101	3D	95	1011111	5F
62	111110	3E	96	1100000	60
63	111111	3F	97	1100001	61
64	1000000	40	98	1100010	62
65	1000001	41	99	1100011	63
66	1000010	42	100	1100100	64
67	1000011	43			
68	1000100	44			
69	1000101	45			
70	1000110	46			
71	1000111	47			
72	1001000	48			
73	1001001	49			
74	1001010	4A			
75	1001011	4B			

A5.2 Table of Powers of 2

n	2^n	n	2^n
−4	0.0625	9	512
−3	0.125	10	1,024
−2	0.25	11	2,048
−1	0.5	12	4,096
0	1.0	13	8,192
1	2	14	16,384
2	4	15	32,768
3	8	16	65,536
4	16	17	131,072
5	32	18	262,144
6	64	19	524,288
7	128	20	1,048,576
8	256		

OTHER BOOKS OF INTEREST

BP66: BEGINNERS GUIDE TO MICROPROCESSORS AND COMPUTING
E. F. Scott, M.Sc., C.Eng., M.I.E.R.E.

As indicated by the title, this book is intended as an introduction to the basic theory and concepts of binary arithmetic, microprocessor operation and machine-language programming.

There are occasions in the text where some background information might be helpful and a glossary is included at the end of the book. The glossary is also intended to be instructive and some terms form an extension to the main text.

The only prior knowledge which has been assumed is very basic arithmetic and an understanding of indices so the book should therefore prove useful for pupils preparing for C.S.E. and O Level examinations as well as to technicians, engineers and hobbyists.

128 pages   *1980*
0 900162 87 2   **£1.75**

BP72: A MICROPROCESSOR PRIMER
E. A. Parr, B.Sc., C.Eng., M.I.E.E.

A newcomer to electronics tends to be overwhelmed when first confronted with articles or books on microprocessors. The problems encountered generally fall into three categories.

Firstly, we have a vast amount of new terminology and it is a sad fact of life that most books or articles assume the reader is familiar with this jargon.

Secondly, there is an understandable impression of being filled with information from a hosepipe with the effect that the reader is able to understand little bits of technology but is unable to stand back and appreciate the whole picture.

Finally, a lot of microprocessor logic appears to be terribly arbitrary.

In an attempt to give a painless approach to computing, this small book will start by designing a small computer and because of its simplicity and logic structure, the language is hopefully easy to learn and understand. The shortcomings of this simple machine will then be discussed and the reader is shown how these can be overcome by changes and additions to the instruction set. In this way, such ideas as relative addressing, index registers, etc. will be developed and it is hoped that these will be seen as logical progressions rather than arbitrary things to be accepted but not understood.

96 pages   *1980*
0 900162 92 9   **£1.75**

ELEMENTS OF ELECTRONICS
BP77: BOOK 4. Microprocessing Systems and Circuits
F. A. Wilson, C.G.I.A., C.Eng., F.I.E.E., F.I.E.R.E., F.B.I.M.

A truly comprehensive guide to the elements of microprocessing systems which really starts at the beginning. Its purpose is to teach the fundamentals so that the reader will understand what it is all about and never feel excluded or bewildered when reading other literature, which all too often, assumes that the world is full of experts.

The way in which all parts of a complete microcomputing system are put together and the idea that programming is an indispensable component is first developed before the many important facets of a system are discussed in detail. The final chapter develops a whole range of circuits yet no fundamental circuit principles are introduced without an explanation in depth.

To accomodate the range of readers' expertise from that of the newcomer to the moderately proficient, some of the more basic studies are contained within appendices to which reference can be made as required. Especially for the beginner is an appendix containing explanations of the relevant electronic fundamentals and it is fortunate that the mathematical ability needed is not nearly as demanding as for some other electronic disciplines.

The book should therefore have appeal for most people. The subject is compelling and the treatment of it, although only considering the "elements", is thorough. Electronic enthusiasts and readers of earlier books will gain much by expanding into this somewhat new and exciting field of switching. Those already versed in programming must certainly benefit from a knowledge of how it all happens. Also, because of the special appendix, people with experience neither of electronics nor of programming will, without doubt, find this an economical and interesting form of initiation into the vast subject of microprocessing.

In fact, the serious reader should become so well acquainted with the fundamental principles that far from wondering how on earth such marvels are accomplished, he or she should actually be able to devise ways of doing the jobs.

256 pages   *1980*
0 900162 97 X   £2.95

BP86: AN INTRODUCTION TO BASIC PROGRAMMING TECHNIQUES
S. Daly, M.B.C.S.

This book is based on the author's own experience in learning Basic and in helping others, mostly beginners, to program and understand the language.

Also included is a program library containing various programs that the author has actually written and run — these are for biorhythms, plotting a graph of y against x, standard deviation, regression, generating a musical note sequence and a card game.

The book is completed by a number of appendices which include test questions and answers on each chapter and a glossary.

96 pages 1981
0 85934 061 9 **£1.95**

BP109: THE ART OF PROGRAMMING THE 1K ZX81
M. James & S. M. Gee

This book shows you how to use the features of the ZX81 in programs that fit into the 1K machine and are still fun to use. In Chapter Two we explain its random number generator and use it to simulate coin tossing and dice throwing and to play pontoon. There is a great deal of fun to be had in Chapter Three, from the patterns you can display using the ZX81's graphics. Its animated graphics capabilities, explored in Chapter Four, have lots of potential for use in games of skill, such as Lunar Lander and Cannon-ball which are given as complete programs. Chapter Five explains PEEK and POKE and uses them to display large characters. The ZX81's timer is explained in Chapter Six and used for a digital clock and a reaction time game. Chapter Seven is about handling character strings and includes three more ready-to-run programs — Hangman, Coded Messages and a number guessing game. In Chapter Eight there are extra programming hints to help you get even more out of your 1K ZX81.

We hope that you'll find that this book rises to the challenge of the ZX81 and that it teaches you enough artful programming for you to be able to go on to develop programs of your very own.

Also please see book number BP114, The Art of Programming the 16K ZX81.

96 pages *1982*
0 85934 084 8 **£1.95**

BP114: THE ART OF PROGRAMMING THE 16K ZX81
M. James & S. M. Gee

This is a companion volume to BP109, *The Art of Programming the 1K ZX81* which introduces the possibilities that are opened up by adding the 16K RAM pack to the ZX81. The topics covered include full screen, scrolling and paged graphics and how to PEEK and POKE characters on to the screen, tape storage and number formatting — which allow you to use your ZX81 for statistics and financial programs — a further discussion on randomness, introducing the idea of simulations and an easy way of calculating π, and methods of designing and debugging a program. The use of the ZX printer is also explained in this book, including upper and lower case character sets, and the final chapter introduces machine code. Plenty of entertaining and useful programs are included.

144 pages *1982*
0 85934 089 9 **£2.50**

BP119: THE ART OF PROGRAMMING THE ZX SPECTRUM
M. James, B.Sc., M.B.C.S.

The incredible ZX Spectrum presents its user with virtually unlimited scope. It allows versatile use of colour, offers high and low resolution graphics and also adds sound. The result can mean some very effective and exciting programs from BASIC – if you just know how!

The problem is that there is a little more than meets the eye in getting your Spectrum to do clever things. It is one thing to have learnt how to use all the Spectrum's commands but a very different one to be able to combine them into programs that do exactly what you want them to. This is just what this book is all about – teaching you the art of effective programming with your Spectrum.

The text is divided into the following chapters: 1, Getting to Know Your Spectrum; 2, Low Resolution Graphics; 3, Fun at Random; 4, High Resolution Graphics; 5, Sound; 6, Moving Graphics; 7, PEEK and POKE; 8, A Sense of Time; 9, Strings and Things; 10, Advanced Graphics.

Essential reading for all Spectrum users be they beginners or seasoned programmers.

144 pages *1983*
0 85934 094 5 **£2.50**

Notes

Notes

Notes

Notes

Please note overleaf is a list of other titles that are available in our range of Radio, Electronics and Computer Books.

These should be available from all good Booksellers, Radio Component Dealers and Mail Order Companies.

However, should you experience difficulty in obtaining any title in your area, then please write directly to the publisher enclosing payment to cover the cost of the book plus adequate postage.

If you would like a complete catalogue of our entire range of Radio, Electronics and Computer Books then please send a Stamped Addressed Envelope to:

BERNARD BABANI (publishing) LTD
THE GRAMPIANS
SHEPHERDS BUSH ROAD
LONDON W6 7NF
ENGLAND

Code	Title	Price
205	First Book of Hi-Fi Loudspeaker Enclosures	95p
221	28 Tested Transistor Projects	1.25p
222	Solid State Short Wave Receivers for Beginners	1.25p
223	50 Projects Using IC CA3130	1.25p
224	50 CMOS IC Projects	1.35p
225	A Practical Introduction to Digital IC's	1.25p
226	How to Build Advanced Short Wave Receivers	1.95p
227	Beginners Guide to Building Electronic Projects	1.95p
228	Essential Theory for the Electronics Hobbyist	1.95p
RCC	Resistor Colour Code Disc	20p
BP1	First Book of Transistor Equivalents and Substitutes	1.50p
BP6	Engineers and Machinists Reference Tables	75p
BP7	Radio and Electronic Colour Codes and Data Chart	40p
BP14	Second Book of Transistor Equivalents and Substitutes	1.75p
BP24	52 Projects Using IC741	1.25p
BP27	Chart of Radio Electronic Semiconductor and Logic Symbols	50p
BP32	How to Build Your Own Metal and Treasure Locators	1.95p
BP33	Electronic Calculator Users Handbook	1.50p
BP34	Practical Repair and Renovation of Colour TVs	1.25p
BP36	50 Circuits Using Germanium, Silicon and Zener Diodes	1.50p
BP37	50 Projects Using Relays, SCR's and TRIACs	1.95p
BP39	50 (FET) Field Effect Transistor Projects	1.75p
BP40	Digital IC Equivalents and Pin Connections	3.50p
BP41	Linear IC Equivalents and Pin Connections	3.50p
BP42	50 Simple L.E.D. Circuits	1.50p
BP43	How to Make Walkie-Talkies	1.95p
BP44	IC555 Projects	1.95p
BP45	Projects in Opto-Electronics	1.95p
BP46	Mobile Discotheque Handbook	1.35p
BP48	Electronic Projects for Beginners	1.95p
BP49	Popular Electronic Projects	1.95p
BP50	IC LM3900 Projects	1.35p
BP51	Electronic Music and Creative Tape Recording	1.95p
BP52	Long Distance Television Reception (TV–DX) for the Enthusiast	1.95p
BP53	Practical Electronic Calculations and Formulae	2.95p
BP55	Radio Stations Guide	1.75p
BP56	Electronic Security Devices	1.95p
BP57	How to Build Your Own Solid State Oscilloscope	1.95p
BP58	50 Circuits Using 7400 Series IC's	1.95p
BP59	Second Book of CMOS IC Projects	1.50p
BP60	Practical Construction of Pre-amps, Tone Controls, Filters & Attn	1.45p
BP61	Beginners Guide to Digital Techniques	95p
BP62	Elements of Electronics – Book 1	2.25p
BP63	Elements of Electronics – Book 2	2.25p
BP64	Elements of Electronics – Book 3	2.25p
BP65	Single IC Projects	1.50p
BP66	Beginners Guide to Microprocessors and Computing	1.75p
BP67	Counter Driver and Numeral Display Projects	1.75p
BP68	Choosing and Using Your Hi-Fi	1.65p
BP69	Electronic Games	1.75p
BP70	Transistor Radio Fault-Finding Chart	50p
BP71	Electronic Household Projects	1.75p
BP72	A Microprocessor Primer	1.75p
BP73	Remote Control Projects	1.95p
BP74	Electronic Music Projects	1.75p
BP75	Electronic Test Equipment Construction	1.75p
BP76	Power Supply Projects	1.75p
BP77	Elements of Electronics – Book 4	2.95p
BP78	Practical Computer Experiments	1.75p
BP79	Radio Control for Beginners	1.75p
BP80	Popular Electronic Circuits – Book 1	1.95p
BP81	Electronic Synthesiser Projects	1.75p
BP82	Electronic Projects Using Solar-Cells	1.95p
BP83	VMOS Projects	1.95p
BP84	Digital IC Projects	1.95p
BP85	International Transistor Equivalents Guide	2.95p
BP86	An Introduction to Basic Programming Techniques	1.95p
BP87	Simple L.E.D. Circuits – Book 2	1.35p
BP88	How to Use Op-Amps	2.25p
BP89	Elements of Electronics – Book 5	2.95p
BP90	Audio Projects	1.95p
BP91	An Introduction to Radio DX-ing	1.95p
BP92	Electronics Simplified – Crystal Set Construction	1.75p
BP93	Electronic Timer Projects	1.95p
BP94	Electronic Projects for Cars and Boats	1.95p
BP95	Model Railway Projects	1.95p
BP96	C B Projects	1.95p
BP97	IC Projects for Beginners	1.95p
BP98	Popular Electronic Circuits – Book 2	2.25p
BP99	Mini-Matrix Board Projects	1.95p
BP100	An Introduction to Video	1.95p
BP101	How to Identify Unmarked IC's	65p
BP102	The 6809 Companion	1.95p
BP103	Multi-Circuit Board Projects	1.95p
BP104	Electronic Science Projects	2.25p
BP105	Aerial Projects	1.95p
BP106	Modern Op-Amp Projects	1.95p
BP107	30 Solderless Breadboard Projects – Book 1	1.95p
BP108	International Diode Equivalents Guide	2.25p
BP109	The Art of Programming the 1K ZX81	1.95p
BP110	How to Get Your Electronic Projects Working	1.95p
BP111	Elements of Electronics – Book 6	3.50p
BP112	A Z-80 Workshop Manual	2.75p
BP113	30 Solderless Breadboard Projects – Book 2	2.25p
BP114	The Art of Programming the 16K ZX81	2.50p
BP115	The Pre-Computer Book	1.95p
BP116	Electronic Toys Games and Puzzles	2.25p
BP117	Practical Electronic Building Blocks – Book 1	2.25p
BP118	Practical Electronic Building Blocks – Book 2	2.25p
BP119	The Art of Programming the ZX Spectrum	2.95p
BP120	Audio Amplifier Fault-Finding Chart	65p
BP121	How to Design and Make Your Own PCBs	2.25p
BP122	Audio Amplifier Construction	2.25p
BP123	A Practical Introduction to Microprocessors	2.25p
BP124	How to Design Electronic Projects	2.25p